ECONOMIC ISSUES, PROBLEMS AND PERSPECTIVES

ADVANCES IN CAPITAL STRUCTURE RESEARCH

Economic Issues, Problems and Perspectives

Additional books and e-books in this series can be found on Nova's website under the Series tab.

ECONOMIC ISSUES, PROBLEMS AND PERSPECTIVES

ADVANCES IN CAPITAL STRUCTURE RESEARCH

KAREL MARLEAU
EDITOR

nova
science publishers
New York

NOTICE TO THE READER

Library of Congress Cataloging-in-Publication Data

Names: Marleau, Karel, editor.
Title: Advances in capital structure research / Karel Marleau (editor).
Description: New York : Nova Science Publishers, [2020] | Series: Economic issues, problems and perspectives | Includes bibliographical references and index. |
Identifiers: LCCN 2021034916 (print) | LCCN 2021034917 (ebook) | ISBN 9781536199482 (paperback) | ISBN 9781536199697 (adobe pdf)
Subjects: LCSH: Capital investments. | Capital costs. | Corporate debt. | Corporations--Finance.
Classification: LCC HG4028.C4 A26 2020 (print) | LCC HG4028.C4 (ebook) | DDC 338.4/3--dc23
LC record available at https://lccn.loc.gov/2021034916
LC ebook record available at https://lccn.loc.gov/2021034917

Published by Nova Science Publishers, Inc. † New York

CONTENTS

Preface

Capital structure refers to the distribution of debt and equity a company uses to finance its overall operations and growth. This four-chapter volume details recent advancements in capital structure research, including perspectives on the global water industry and European banks as well as an analysis of SME financing behavior and a systematic literature review.

Chapter 1 - Water may be our most basic and precious resource. However, climate change and severe weather extremes affect water resources around the world in coming years. As changing climate had led to water shortages in many places, there is an urgently need to expand water utilities, water infrastructure and water treatment plants while protecting water resources as well. Thus, investment in water is critical and private funding is a proper way to meet the financial needs in the water industry. In this book chapter, the authors examine the determinants of capital structure of 72 private water companies (water utilities, water infrastructure and water treatment plants) that comprise the 4 water indices (WOWAX, S-NET, S&P and MSCI ACWI) over the world for the period of 2004-2014 using unbalanced panel (fixed effects) regression model for the financing decision focuses. The eight attributes' variables (Profitability, size, age, risk, free cash flows, tangibility asset, non-debt tax shield and growth opportunity) are used to explain the capital structure (Leverage, long-term debt to asset and short-term debt to asset. This study uses unbalanced panel (fixed effects) regression model. The authors' results show that these eight attributes' variables positively and negatively impact on capital structure at the 1%, 5% and 10% levels of significance, respectively. The findings would be useful to higher level executives of water companies' who may tend to favour optimal capital structure to increase the profitability and thus distribute more dividends to shareholders than other variables.

Chapter 2 - Research on firm capital structure and macroeconomic conditions has gained momentum in recent years, particularly following the 2007-2008 global financial crisis. Similarly, the recent macroeconomic downturn due to the COVID-19 pandemic and the subsequent corporate liquidity problems highlight the importance of a comprehensive analysis of corporate financing issues under different macroeconomic conditions. However, what do we know about the relationship between firm capital structure and macroeconomic events? This chapter aims to answer this question via a systematic literature review (SLR) to highlight the key contributors, the key areas of investigation and the main results in the literature and to ultimately suggest a future research agenda for the field. Based on a comprehensive sample of 156 articles published from 1992 to 2020 and retrieved from the Web of Science (WoS) database, the authors apply an SLR and a bibliometric analysis to investigate the main characteristics of the literature on the relationship between firm capital structure and different macroeconomic states. Specifically, the authors highlight the evolution of this path of research over the years and the most influential authors, types of publications, and journals. Moreover, the authors identify the main research areas in the field. The first area of research focuses on the adjustment of the debt/equity level under different macroeconomic conditions. The determinants of firm capital structure in different macroeconomic states represent the second area of research. The main research gaps and the future research agenda are also discussed.

Chapter 3 - This chapter seeks to analyse SME financing behaviour regarding the adjustment toward the target short-term debt ratio. To reach the paper's objective, using dynamic panel data models, the authors consider a sample of 8787 SMEs of the manufacturing sector for the period between 2010 and 2017. The results suggest that these firms, after the exhaustion of funds generated internally, rely on short-term debt. The deviation costs seem to imply a fast speed of adjustment to rebalance the short-term debt ratio, avoiding short-term financing imbalance in order to renegotiate credit on favourable terms. The results show that distance from the target short-term debt ratio impacts negatively on the speed of adjustment toward that target ratio. This negative relationship suggests that SMEs distant from the target short-term debt ratio bear transaction costs higher than deviation costs, presenting financing imbalance in the short-run.

Chapter 4 - Since the beginning of the European banking integration in November 2014, debt structure has become essential in the bank capitalization process. This chapter discusses the way in which debt structure (short- and long-term) affects capitalization, risk management and, consequently, the business model of banks. The apparent disconnection between the market valuation of risky assets held by banks and their book value is investigated through the cross-use of market variables against more standard accounting data. In order to better understand the type of restructuring now under way in the major European Banks, the authors run a Panel OLS to analyze the capitalization process using a broad panel of 133 banks covering the period 2000-2017, and a smaller sample composed of the largest institutions. The authors' finding is that both short- and long-term debt has a major effect on bank capitalization. The most vulnerable institutions are those with substantial levels of short-term debt and significant volumes of non-performing assets. Long-term debt, in contrast, allows banks to be more resilient. Regulators should therefore pay particular attention to the way banks handle their volumes of non-performing loans to ensure overall stability.

In: Advances in Capital Structure Research ISBN: 978-1-53619-948-2
Editor: Karel Marleau

Chapter 1

THE DETERMINANTS OF CAPITAL STRUCTURE: EVIDENCE FROM THE GLOBAL WATER INDUSTRY

Rajibur Reza[1*] and Gurudeo Anand Tularam[2]

[1]Department of Accounting, Finance and Economics, Griffith University, Nathan campus, Australia

[2]Mathematics and Statistics Senior Researcher, Science, Griffith University, Nathan campus, Australia

ABSTRACT

Water may be our most basic and precious resource. However, climate change and severe weather extremes affect water resources around the world in coming years. As changing climate had led to water shortages in many places, there is an urgently need to expand water utilities, water infrastructure and water treatment plants while protecting water resources as well. Thus, investment in water is critical and private funding is a proper way to meet the financial needs in the water industry. In this book chapter, we examine the determinants of capital structure of 72 private water companies (water utilities, water infrastructure and water treatment

* Corresponding Author's E-mail: smrajibur.reza@griffithuni.edu.au.

plants) that comprise the 4 water indices (WOWAX, S-NET, S&P and MSCI ACWI) over the world for the period of 2004-2014 using unbalanced panel (fixed effects) regression model for the financing decision focuses. The eight attributes' variables (Profitability, size, age, risk, free cash flows, tangibility asset, non-debt tax shield and growth opportunity) are used to explain the capital structure (Leverage, long-term debt to asset and short-term debt to asset. This study uses unbalanced panel (fixed effects) regression model. Our results show that these eight attributes' variables positively and negatively impact on capital structure at the 1%, 5% and 10% levels of significance, respectively. The findings would be useful to higher level executives of water companies' who may tend to favour optimal capital structure to increase the profitability and thus distribute more dividends to shareholders than other variables.

Keywords: investment, private water companies', capital structure, water industry, financing decision

INTRODUCTION

Water may be our most basic and precious resource (Reza et al., 2017; Hassan and Tularam, 2018) but interest and research on water security are rapidly growing issue around the world. It is well known that water is under threat and may in fact run out in many places around the world. This is because around 80% of the people in our world have been difficulty accessing safe drinking water (Roca et al. 2015; Reza et al., 2017). More specifically, approximately 2 billion people (29 percent world's population) over the world do not access to sufficient drinking water, and over 4 billion (55 per cent) people have been affecting by water scarcities for at least 1 month per year (Mekonnen and Hoekstra, 2016; Tularam and Reza, 2016). This may be due to the increases in the world's population and thus leading to water demand unavoidably increasing - the world population is projected to grow by 34 percent from 7 billion today to 9.1 billion in 2050 (Roca and Tularam, 2012; Vandone et al. 2018).

The main socio-economic factors that drive increasing water demand are population growth, and dramatically increasing urbanization in countries (Tularam and Murali 2015; Tularam and Hassan 2016; Reza et al., 2017). In terms of the population growth and urbanization, there is little uncertainty about changes on levels of water supply stress (Tularam and Ilahee, 2010; Reza and Tularam, 2017) but concerning climate change and severe weather extremes weather patterns being noted in recent times suggest the stress on the water resources around the world would be highly increased in coming years (Tularam and Reza, 2017; Tularam and Hassan 2016). The research on the changing climate suggests that climate led to water shortages has been occurring so there is a need to challenge ourselves to adapt to the change in conditions – that is, attempt to balance water supply and water demand in parts of the world, particularly South Asia, Sub-Saharan Africa as well as some parts of Northern Europe (Tularam and Reza, 2016; Roca et al., 2015).

In an attempt to address the water scarcity problems projected for the future, the United Nations has adopted Sustainable Development Goals[1]. To achieve the ambitious SDG Goal, 6[2] targets were developed to improve the water use efficiency through more sustainable investments. McKinsey Global Institute (2013)[3] stated that as large as USD 12 trillion may be needed for the upgrading of the global water infrastructure and this would need to be completed by 2030. Currently, the water infrastructure spending requirement of the developing countries is around USD 114 billion, only to ensure access to drinking water for all[4]. Evidently, there is a large gap in the financing of water investments as required in relation to the current investments that have been flowing in the water infrastructure - treatment plants and utilities. Further, Sachwani (2020) advocates that USD 1.7 trillion would be urgent needed to invest for water supply and sanitation. However, if the water industry fails to invest this amount of money, this industry could be reduced 6% (approximately) GDP growth rates by 2050. For the above reasons, there is an urgent need to expand water utilities, water infrastructure and water treatment plants to enhance the water supply to all areas (Reza, 2017; Jin et al., 2014).

Clearly, the public sector water funds are rather limited and due to the insufficient investments from public sector, much private investment

---

[1] https://www.undp.org/sustainable-development-goals

[2] ttps://www.undp.org/sustainable-development-goals#clean-water-and-sanitation

[3] https://www.mckinsey.com/mgi/overview

[4]https://www.webuildvalue.com/en/global-economy-sustainability/water-infrastructure.html

is needed and appears to be the only way to appropriately fund the large gap in the water sector. This could be done through various forms such as asset sales, concession contracts and lease contracts (Jin et al., 2014; Jin et al., 2015; Reza, 2017). In this process of change, during the early 2000s, several of water-related indices, water funds and water exchange traded funds (ETFs) were formed; that is, to works towards acceptances of the water stocks as an alternative investment asset i.e., water is to be treated as an investment commodity (Reza, 2017; Roca et al., 2015). Thus, investors can take a position in or out of the water indices - World Water Index (WOWAX), S-Network Global Water Index (S-Net), S&P Global Water Index (S&P), MSCI ACWI Water Utilities Index (MSCI ACWI), ISE Water Index, NASDAQ OMX Global Water Index and NASDAQ OMX US; water funds (see, for instance, Pictet Global Water Fund, SAM Sustainable Water Fund etc.) and water ETFs such as Invesco Water Resources ETF (PHO), Invesco Global Water ETF (PIO), First Trust Water ETF (FIW) and Invesco S&P Global Water Index ETF (CGW)

Given that private financing is then essential for private water companies to enhance the project for water supply, it is essential to search for diverse sources, which can play a vital role in financing decisions - such as issuing equity or bond, debt to investors for long-term financial capability and so on (Jin et al., 2014). Essentially, water companies can borrow short-term or long-term bank loan to fill the financing gap. In this case, capital structure is an important tool for financial decision-making ability to obtain funding with debts and equity (Reza and Tularam, 2017; Jin, 2015).

According to Sikveland and Zhang (2020), "Capital structure is an important determinant of a firm's overall risk profile. A high debt ratio can make the cycles in profitability even more pronounced as debt can contribute to increasing profitability in good times and reduce it in economic downturns…" (p. 1). It is possible for water company management personnel to maximize the value of water companies through capital structure decision making. In this study, we investigate the determinants of the capital structure of 72 private water companies worldwide. Further, we study the factors that influence the financing policy decisions of water companies in relation to the different funding sources.

To the author's knowledge, to date no study has analysed the determinants of capital structure of the private water companies as done in this study. So, this study contributes to the knowledge on capital structure by considering important factors in the determinants of capital structure of private water companies. In terms of the investor, this analysis and results of this study may provide a "deeper" understanding of the capital structure and how it is then related to the volatility and returns of a water company.

The rest of this chapter is organized as follows: Section 2 focuses on the theoretical framework and literature review, while Section 3 describes the methodology employed, and Section 4 reports and discusses the results; and finally, Section 5 concludes the study.

THEORETICAL FRAMEWORK AND LITERATURE REVIEW

According to Abor and Biekpe (2009), "Capital Structure is defined as a specific mixture of debt and equity a firm uses to finance its operations..." (p. 84). The theory of capital structure has been a bewildering issue in the corporate finance literature since 1958. Modigliani and Miller (1958) introduced the theory of "capital structure irrelevance", which is well known. These authors were unable to discern exactly how financial leverage affects firms' performance. Their theory has been criticized because, in reality, there are no perfect capital markets. Modigliani and Miller (1963) revised their early theory by incorporating tax benefit and they argue that market imperfection is a determinant of the capital structure of firms. Although Modigliani and Miller's theory is criticized by researchers, their theory makes some sense in relation to the research on capital structure. The four major theories of capital structure are the trade-off theory, the agency costs theory, the pecking order theory, and the market timing theory.

According to the trade-off theory (Kraus and Litzenberger 1973; Myers 1984), costs and benefits of debt and equity financing could be associated with taxes, bankruptcy costs and agency costs. Jensen and Meckling (1976) expanded and developed the agency costs theory, which contends that target conflicts exist between managers and shareholders (agency cost of equity) or between shareholders and debt holders (agency cost of debt). Jensen (1986) argues that managers are under pressure from high debt levels until they are able to create cash flow to pay their interest. Hence, surplus cash can reduce agency costs. In contrast to the trade-off theory, Myers and Majluf (1984) developed the pecking order theory, based on the notion of transaction costs, issuing costs and asymmetric information between firms' managers and investors. They state that the pecking order theory is a hierarchy of financing, i.e., retained earnings is used first, then debt is issued, and finally new shares are issued. More recently, Baker and Wurgler (2002) introduced the market timing theory of capital structure. The authors state that "equity market timing refers to the practice of issuing shares at high prices and repurchasing at low prices…" (p.1). Thus, using this theory, firm managers could increase current shareholder's wealth and there is no notion of optimal capital structure to maximize firm value.

Although Modigliani and Miller's theory is criticized by researchers, major research work on capital structure originates from the work of Modigliani and Miller (1958), which has led to the emergence of various theories of capital structure over the last five decades.

In the finance literature, several studies have been conducted on the determinants of capital structure (see, for instance, Modigliani and Miller, 1958, 1963, Jensen and Meckling, 1976, Myers and Majluf, 1984; Titman and Wessels, 1988; Harris and Raviv, 1991; Baker and Wurgler, 2002; Chen, 2004; Zhang, 2010; Sangeetha and Sivathaasan, 2013; Vo, 2017; Orlova et al., 2020).

In terms of capital structure, Akhtar (2005) investigates the determinants of capital structure of Australian multinational and domestic corporations for the period of 1992 to 2001 using Tobit model. She finds that that the level of leverage significance is the same between multinational and domestic corporations. Similarly, Akhtar and Oliver (2009) study the determinants of capital structure of Japanese multinational and domestic corporations. Their results show that the level of leverage, age, collateral value of assets, free cash flows, foreign exchange risks, growth, non-debt tax shields, political risks, profitability and size of Japanese multinational differ significantly between Japanese multinational and domestic corporations. However, they do not find that business risks of Japanese multinational differ are not significant between Japanese multinational and domestic corporations. Further,

Akhtar (2017) compares the capital structure in multinational corporations (MCs) and domestic corporations (DCs) in Australia, U.S., Japan, U.K. and Malaysia for the period of 1995-2013. She points out that the debt practices capacity varies between DCs and MCs. Importantly, Australia, Japan, U.K; and Malaysian MCs borrow less long-term debt relative than U.S. firms.

In contrast, Abor and Biekpe (2009) examine the determinants of capital structure decisions of small and medium enterprises (SMEs) in Ghana. They find that firm's age, size, asset structure, profitability, and growth influences the capital structure of Ghanaian SMEs. Similarly, Balio et al. (2016) study the determinants of capital structure decisions of SMEs in Greece. Their results support Abor and Biekpe (2009) in that they confirm that size, growth, asset structure and profitability all influence the capital structure of Greek SMEs,

Using panel regression model, Alipour et al. (2015) study the determinants of capital structure of manufacturing firms in Iran and find that Short-term debt plays a vital role for financing source of Iranian corporations. Phooi M'ng et al. (2017) examine the determinants of capital structure of Malaysia, Singapore, and Thailand for the period of 2004 to 2013. They find that profitability negatively impacts a firm's profitability in Malaysia and Singapore; but an insignificant influence is noted for Thailand, while Ramli et al. (2019) investigate the determinants of capital structure for the period of 1990–2010 to find out that there is a positive relationship between capital structure and firm profitability in Malaysia and Indonesia.

Recently, Cai et al. (2019) have studied the determinants of capital structure in PPP infrastructure projects across 22 countries using generalized least-squares (GLS) regression model. They noted three project-specific factors - number of sponsors, number of lenders, and contract type, as well as four country-specific factors; namely, total tax rate, real interest rate, risk premium on lending, and bond market capitalization are positively significant with capital structure. Sikveland and Zhang (2020) have studied Norwegian salmon farming industry for the period of 2001 to 2014 from which they reported that the Norwegian listed aquaculture firms had lower total debt, long-term debt and short-term debt and higher liquidity than non-listed aquaculture firms.

In the water investment and finance literature, some few studies have been conducted on risk and returns in the water industry (see, for instance, Antoniou et al., 2000; Morana and Sawkins, 2000; Buckland and Fraser, 2001; Pescetto, 2008; Buckland et al., 2015; Jin et al., 2015; Roca and Tularam, 2012; Jin et al., 2015 and 2019; Roca et al., 2015; Tularam and Reza, 2016; Reza et al. 2017 and 2018; Piñeiro-Chousa et al., 2020). However, in terms of capital structure of private water companies, only one study has been completed by Reza and Tularam (2017). These authors investigate the association between ownership structure and capital structure of 72 water companies that consist of the 4 water indices (WOWAX, S-NET, S&P and MSCI ACWI) over the period 2004-2014 using unbalanced panel (random effects) regression model. Their results confirm that foreign ownership impacts on leverage and short-term debt at the 10% and 1% level of significance. However, they find that there is no relationship between institutional ownership, and the leverage and short-term debt. This brief review of the literature review shows the research gaps on the determinate of the capital structure of the global water industry. This study addresses this aspect and extends the work to examine the existence of the determination of capital structure on private water companies worldwide. It is important to note that one report[5] is produced in 2002 by the Water Services Regulation Authority (OFWAT) for UK private water utilities (the report was not a peer reviewed paper).

DATA AND METHODOLOGY

Data

We test eight indicators – profitability (PROFIT), size (SIZE), age (AGE), risk (RISK). free cash flows (FCF), tangible asset (TANG), non-debt tax shield (NDTS) and growth opportunities (GROWTH) to how these factors impact on the 72 water companies' (water utilities, water infrastructure and water treatment plants) capital structure variables –

[5]https://www.oxera.com/wp-content/uploads/2018/03/Ofwat-capital-structure-of-Water-Companies.pdf

leverage (LEV), long-term debt to asset (LTD) and short-term debt to asset (STD) that are comprised four water indices – WOWAX, S-Net, S&P and MSCI ACWI. These 72 water companies are listed in different stock exchanges throughout the world such as the Shanghai Stock Exchange, Tokyo Stock Exchange, Korea Stock Exchange, Philippine Stock Exchange, Stock Exchange of Singapore, London Stock Exchange, New York Stock Exchange, Brazil Stock Exchange, Euro Next Paris, and Helsinki Stock Exchange. We obtain capital structure and eight attributes' variables for the period of 1 January 2004 to 31 December 2014 (11–years period) from Bloomberg and Reuters DataStream database. This sample period is selected as the WOWAX were formed in January 2004. However, the most of the water indices has been started since 2002.

Empirical Model

In terms of time series, to examine the determinants of the capital structure of private water companies in the WOWAX, S-Net, S&P and MSCI ACWI, this study employs the unbalanced panel (Fixed effects) regression model by Reza (2017). The general form of the Fixed effects model can be conducted is given as:

Model 1

$$\mathrm{LEV_{it}} = \beta_0 + \beta_1\mathrm{PROFIT_{it}} + \beta_2\mathrm{SIZE_{it}} + \beta_3\mathrm{AGE_{it}} + \beta_4\mathrm{RISK}_{\mathrm{it}} + \beta_5\mathrm{FCF_{it}} + \beta_6\mathrm{TANG_{it}} + \beta_7\mathrm{NDTS}_{\mathrm{it}} + \beta_8\mathrm{GROWTH_{it}} + \varepsilon_t \quad (1)$$

Model 2

$$\mathrm{LTD_{it}} = \beta_0 + \beta_1\mathrm{PROFIT_{it}} + \beta_2\mathrm{SIZE_{it}} + \beta_3\mathrm{AGE_{it}} + \beta_4\mathrm{RISK}_{\mathrm{it}} + \beta_5\mathrm{FCF_{it}} + \beta_6\mathrm{TANG_{it}} + \beta_7\mathrm{NDTS}_{\mathrm{it}} + \beta_8\mathrm{GROWTH_{it}} + \varepsilon_t \quad (2)$$

Model 3

$$STD_{it} = \beta_0 + \beta_1 PROFIT_{it} + \beta_2 SIZE_{it} + \beta_3 AGE_{it} + \beta_4 RISK_{it} + \beta_5 FCF_{it} + \beta_6 TANG_{it} + \beta_7 NDTS_{it} + \beta_8 GROWTH_{it} + \varepsilon_t \quad (3)$$

where i and t symbolize water company and time respectively and ε_t is the random error component. Equations (1), (2) and (3) advocate that the decision to determination of capital structure depends on eight attributes variables of 72 water companies. Eight attributes' variables - PROFIT, SIZE, AGE, RISK. FCF, TANG, NDTS and GROWTH are independent variables. LEV, LTD and STD are dependent variables, LEV is measured by total debt is divided by total assets (Reza and Tularam, 2017). LTD is defined as the ratio of long-term debt to asset (Vo., 2017). STD is calculated by short-term debt divided by total assets ((Reza and Tularam, 2017). The following sub-section provides independent variables definition and hypothesis.

Independent Variables and Hypotheses

Specifically, this study investigates the nature of the reciprocal relationship between capital structure and financial variables of the global water companies and the consequent effect of this relationship on the capital structure determinants. The study poses the following main question: "What are the main factors or variables that influence different capital structures of water companies?"

It is important to note that capital structure is difficult to evaluate and equally the types of investments and growth opportunities that are likely to be associated with insider and outsider shareholders are as difficult to anlayse. According to Ebaid (2009), capital structure could be explained by two dominant theories: the trade-off theory and the pecking order theory as noted.

For this study, both trade-off and pecking order theories are assumed, and based on this a number of financial factors/variables are considered. The variables selected are those that normally influence a firm's financial decision making, and it is assumed that these decisions are made by managers using the trade-off theory and pecking order theory.

This study empirically investigates the impact of factors or variables on water companies' capital structure. On the basis of theoretical analyses and available empirical evidence (Abor and Biekpe, 2009), this study seeks to test the following hypotheses regarding the structure of water companies in an attempt to answer the research question posed earlier.

Profitability

Profitability (PROFIT) is the measurement of firm financial gain which depends on firm business operations. According to Myers (1984), firms prefer raising capital due to the costs of issuing new equity. Hence, a firm's first preference concerns retained earnings, second preference debt, and third preference issuing new equity. It is noted that the amount of earnings is available from retained (Titman, 1988). Thus, PROFIT is an important determinant of the capital structure. We use return on asset (ROA) which is calculated by examining the ratios of net income and total asset (Reza and Tularam, 2017) - for PROFIT measurement.

According to the pecking order theory, a negative relationship exists between PROFIT and LEV, LTD and STD (see, Titman and Wessels, 1988; Shyam-Sunder and Myers, 1999; Fama and French, 2002; Frank and Goyal, 2009; Arvanitis et al., 2012; Sikveland and Zhang, 2020). However, several prior studies (Dammon and Senbet, 1988; Al-Ajmi et al., 2009; Zhang, 2010, Mateeva et al., 2013; Sangeetha and Sivathaasan, 2013; Balios et al., 2016; Phooi M'ng et al., 2017) claim a positive link with PROFIT and LEV, LTD and STD, support the trade-off theory. Therefore, we test the following hypotheses separately.

The first hypothesis is:

H_{01}: There is no relationship between PROFIT and capital structure.

H_{1a}: There is a positive relationship between PROFIT and capital structure.

H_{1b}: There is a negative relationship between PROFIT and capital structure.

Size

Firm size (SIZE) is calculated by determining the natural logarithm of total assets (Abor and Biekpe, 2009). The claim is that the size is an important financial variable that helps determine the capital structure of firms in many different perspectives (Titman and Wessels, 1988; Vo, 2017). Titman and Wessels (1988) claim that larger firms tend to be more diversified and have lower chance to ruin. Subsequently, larger firms are treated as highly leveraged firms (Titman and Wessels, 1988; Abor and Biekpe, 2009; Vo, 2017). Issue cost of equity and debt are related to firm SIZE. Usually, small firms pay more money than large firms for issuing new equity as well as pay more money to issue LTD. Hence, small firms are treated as more leveraged than large firms. For this reason, the small firms prefer to borrow short term loan instead of long-term loan whereas the large firms prefer long-term debt.

According to trade-off theory, a number of authors (Rajan and Zingales, 1995; Michaelas et al. 1999; Sogorb-Mira, 2005; Abor and Biekpe, 2009; Frank and Goyal, 2009; Zhang, 2010; Cortez and Susanto, 2012; Sangeetha and Sivathaasan, 2013; Vo, 2017; Ramli et al., 2019) have noted a positive relationship between SIZE and capital structure, Further, according to the pecking order theory, some find a negative relationship between firm SIZE and capital structure (see, Kester, 1986; Titman and Wessels, 1988; Hall et al. 2004; Chakraborty, 2010; Vo, 2017). Hence, we test the following hypothesis.

The second hypothesis is:

H_0: There is no relationship between SIZE and capital structure.

H_{2a}: There is a positive relationship between SIZE and capital structure.

H_{2b}: There is a negative relationship between SIZE and capital structure.

Age

Age (AGE) is a standard measure for firm reputation as it is important if a firm is to take on more debt (Abor and Biekpe, 2009). The Firm AGE is currently an important financial variable that helps determine the firm's capital structure. AGE is defined as the number of years of a firm from date of incorporation (Reza and Tularam, 2017). The trade-off theory claims a positive association between the firm AGE and LEV whereas pecking order theory suggests the alternative assumption i.e., an older firm generally use less debt over time. Hence, there is a higher LEV for an older firm. Akhtar and Oliver (2009) note that AGE comprises agency costs, default risks and information asymmetries. They also point out that an older firm usually experiences lower default risks due to steady profits. Hence, the third hypothesis of this study is as follows:

H_0: There is no relationship between AGE and capital structure.

H_{3a}: There is a positive relationship between AGE and capital structure.

H_{3b}: There is a negative relationship between AGE and capital structure.

Risk

The risk (RISK) variable is one of the determinants of a firm's capital structure (Kale et al., 1991; Abor and Biekpe, 2009). This variable concerns the uncertainty of future stock returns and risk. RISK is calculated as the standard deviation of the stock returns in a given year (Reza and Tularam, 2017). The percentage in terms of standard deviation changes influences the operating income (Titman and Wessels, 1988). A few studies (Michaelas et al., 1999; Chen, 2004; Nguyen and Ramachandran, 2006; Kaur and Rao, 2009) have positive associations between RISK and LEV.

However, Al-Ajmi et al. (2009) shows that firm RISK is negatively related to LEV. Further, Esperanca et al. (2003) find that positive associations between RISK, LTD and STD. Hence, we test the following hypothesis:

H_0: There is no relationship between RISK and capital structure.

H_{4a}: There is a positive relationship between RISK and capital structure.

H_{4b}: There is a negative relationship between RISK and capital structure.

Free Cash Flows

Free cash flows (FCF) is defined as the operating net income before depreciation expenses, less corporate income tax, interest expenses and cash dividends (Reza and Tularam, 2017). Following Jensen (1986), Akhtar and Oliver (2009) state that "excess free cash flow is cash flow in excess of that required to fund all projects that have positive net present value..." (p. 7). Usually, a firm faces agency problem between shareholders and managers for high level of FCF. For low level FCF, a firm can reduce agency cost of debt by utilizing the extra cash flow for long-term debt interest payments (Akthar, 2017). Further, Orlova et al. (2020) find that FCF negatively impact on capital structure. However, Akthar (2017) shows that Japanese firms FCF have a positive relationship with Leverage whereas Australian firms FCF are negative with leverage. Hence, we test the following hypothesis.

H_0: There is no relationship between FCF and capital structure.

H_{5a}: There is a positive relationship between FCF and capital structure.

H_{5b}: There is a negative relationship between FCF and capital structure.

Tangible Asset

Both the agency theory and trade-off theory suggest that tangible asset (TANG) is also an important determinant of capital structure (Abor and Biekpe, 2009; Vo, 2017). TANG is defined as fixed tangible assets divided by the total assets (Akhtar, 2005). Such firms with high intangible assets access to borrow more funds by issuing debt secured (Akhtar, 2005; Abor and Biekpe, 2009). In the similar line of opinions, according to the pecking order theory, Frank and Goyal (2003) state that higher TANG firms are able to borrow more funds with debt security. They argue that a positive relationship exists between TANG and capital structure. Previous studies shows that TANG is positively correlated with LEV (Chen, 2004; Cortez and Susanto, 2012; Sikveland and Zhang. 2020), LTD (see, 2005; Abor and Biekpe, 2009; Vo, 2017; Sikveland and Zhang. 2020) and STD (Esperanc¸a et al., 2003). Nevertheless, a negative relationship has also been noted between tangible asset and LEV (see, Booth et al., 2001; Al-Fayoumi and Abuzayed, 2009; Alipour et al, 2015) LTD (see, Alipour et al., 2015) and STD (Sogorb-Mira, 2005; Abor and Biekpe, 2009; Fauzi et al. 2013; Vo, 2017; Sikveland and Zhang, 2020). Hence, we test the following hypothesis.

The six hypothesis is:

H_0: There is no relationship between TANG and capital structure.

H_{6a}: There is a positive relationship between TANG and capital structure.

H_{6b}: There is a negative relationship between TANG and capital structure.

Non-Debt Tax Shield

Non-debt tax shield (NDTS) is defined as total annual depreciation expense divided by total assets (Titman and Wessels, 1988; Akhtar, 2005; Fauzi et al., 2013). Chakraborty (2010) state that firms prefer to use debt as NDTS with interest as a tax benefit. DeAngelo and Masulis (1980) provide an outline whether tax deductions are not related with debt financing because substitutes are tax deductions for depreciation and investment tax credits for the tax benefits of debt act (Akhtar and Oliver, 2009; Fauzi et al., 2013). As a result, firms with large non-debt tax shields relative to their expected cash flow include less debt in their capital structured. Some of the previous studies find that NDTS is positively correlated with LEV (such as Chakraborty, 2010), LTD (Akhtar, 2017) and STD (such as Fauzi et al., 2013). Yet, a negative relationship has been noted between NDTS and leverage (see, Chen 2004; Akhtar and Oliver, 2009; Ramli et al., 2019) LTD (see, Fauzi et al., 2013) and STD (see, Chen 2004). To understand the context better we test the seventh hypothesis as follows:

H_0: There is no relationship between NDTS and capital structure.

H_{7a}: There is a positive relationship between NDTS and capital structure.

H_{7b}: There is a negative relationship between NDTS and capital structure.

Growth Opportunities

Growth opportunities (GROWTH) is calculated by determining the percentage growth in depreciation adjusted total assets from end of year t-2 to end of year t-1 (Reza and Tularam, 2017). Based on the agency theory ground of capital structure, less debt for financing makes higher GROWTH for a firm, which can be used to reduce the conflict of interest between the debt holders and shareholders (Myers, 1977; Ramli et al., 2019). Larger GROWTH indicates the healthy business performance and based on this aspect a firm is able to access or borrow funds from the financial institutions in the following years. Hence, this would suggest that there is a negative association between GROWTH and higher leverage (Abor and Biekpe, 2009; Vo, 2017). The previous studies (Titman and Wessels, 1988; Michaelas et al., 1999; Sogorb-Mira, 2005; Abor and Biekpe, 2009; Al-Ajmi et al. 2009; Sangeetha and Sivathaasan, 2013; Sikveland and Zhang, 2020) find that GROWTH has positive relationship with the capital structure; according to the pecking order.

Other researchers (Long and Malitz, 1985; Kaur and Rao, 2009; Nunkoo and Boateng, 2010; Zhang, 2010) also note a negative relationship between growth opportunities and capital structure according to the trade-off theory. Hence, we test the following hypothesis eighth as follows:

H_0: There is no relationship between GROWTH and capital structure.

H_{8a}: There is a positive relationship between GROWTH and capital structure.

H_{8b}: There is a negative relationship between GROWTH and capital structure.

The choice of dependent and independent variables and their explanations are provided in Table 1. These variables are used to determine their importance in the capital structure using the fixed effects model.

Table 1. Definition of the variables

Variable	Notation	Description
Leverage	LEV	Total debt divided by total assets
Long-term debt to total assets	LTD	Long-term debt to total assets
Short-term debt to total assets	STD	Short-term debt to total assets
Profitability	PROFIT	Net income divided by total asset
Size	SIZE	Natural logarithm of total assets
Age	AGE	Number of years a firm from date of incorporation
Risk	RISK	Standard deviation of stock return
Free cash flow	FCF	Operating net income before depreciation expenses, less corporate income tax, interest expenses and cash dividends
Tangible assets	TANG	Fixed tangible assets divided by the total assets
Non-debt tax shield	NDTS	Total annual depreciation expense divided by total assets
Growth opportunities	GROWTH	Percentage growth in depreciation-adjusted total assets from end of year t-2 to end of year t-1

RESULTS

Descriptive Statistics

Table 2 exhibits the descriptive statistics of dependent and independent variables of this study.

Descriptive statistics results show that mean returns are positive for all dependent and independent variables. The mean value of leverage is 2.671, with a range of 0 to 0.99, suggesting that all firms have leverage close to the average leverage of water industry. The mean value for LTD is lower than that for STD; indicating firms have more short-term loan. From Table 2, we can see that the FCF has the highest positive mean return (129.854). Mean results are summarized as a graph in Figure 1.

Table 2. Descriptive Statistics

Variable	Mean	Standard Deviation	Minimum	Maximum
LEV	2.671	1.453	-4.057	4.424
LTD	0.198	0.152	-0.092	0.747
STD	0.050	0.063	0.000	0.443
PROFIT	5.150	7.991	-70.100	38.440
SIZE	79.996	461.853	-7.727	4918.794
AGE	3.643	0.932	0.000	5.476
RISK	14.661	26.027	0.000	266.347
FCF	129.854	340.949	-1029.690	3160.900
TANG	26.742	23.771	0.000	91.005
NDTS	0.644	3.641	0.000	36.385
GROWTH	18.949	113.768	-65.414	2198.446

Notes: This table provides the descriptive statistics of dependent (LEV, LTD and STD) and independent (PROFIT, SIZE, AGE, RISK. FCF, TANG, NDTS and GROWTH) variables. Descriptive statistics include daily mean, standard deviation maximum and minimum, See Table 5.1 for variable definitions.

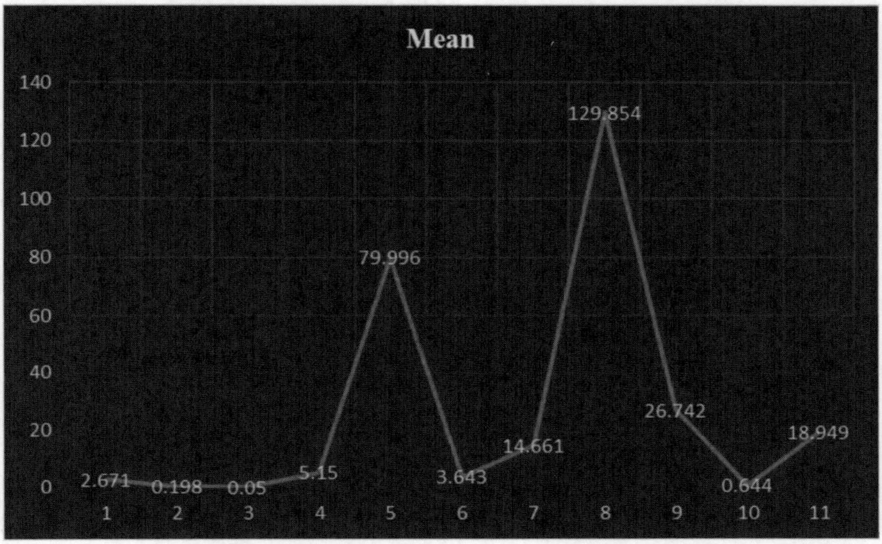

Figure 1. Movements of mean.

Correlation Matrix

Table 3 presents the correlation matrix between dependent and independent variables. Table 3 provides that the correlation coefficients between the capital structure (LEV, LTD and STD) and the eight attributes' variables are both positive and negative. LEV of water companies is positively correlated with SIZE, RISK, FCF, TANG and GROWTH whereas negatively correlated with PROFIT, AGE, NDTS and LTD is negatively correlated with al variables except TANG and GROWTH. STD is negatively correlated with SIZE, RISK, TANG and GROWTH and negatively correlated with PROFIT, AGE, FCF and NDTS. It is important to note that the correlation coefficients result between independent variables do not exceed 0.8. Hence, the results are line with Bryman and Cramer (1997). Additionally, in a multivariate setting, the average variance inflation factor (VIF) statistic for all variables are not more than 4.8; and indeed, far from 10, which indicates that multicollinearity is not important among the independent variables.

Table 3. Correlation matrix

Variable	LEV	LTD	STD	PROFIT	SIZE	AGE	RISK	FCF	TANG	NDTX	GROWTH
LEV	1										
LTD	0.642	1									
STD	0.261	-0.062	1								
PROFIT	-0.088	-0.058	-0.149	1							
SIZE	0.047	-0.005	0.002	0.012	1						
AGE	-0.211	-0.242	-0.088	0.266	0.069	1					
RISK	0.025	-0.088	0.261	-0.164	-0.090	-0.123	1				
FCF	0.032	-0.032	-0.078	0.145	0.009	0.062	-0.014	11			
TANG	0.116	0.199	0.035	0.120	-0.077	-0.094	-0.033	- 0.088	1		
NDTS	-0.061	-0.033	-0.072	0.184	0.000	0.210	-0.001	0.038	0.004	1	
GROWTH	0.066	0.149	0.021	-0.028	-0.016	-0.132	0.054	- 0.054	-0.079	-0.021	1

Notes: This table provides correlation results among dependent (LEV, LTD and STD), independent (PROFIT, SIZE, AGE, RISK. FCF, TANG, NDTS and GROWTH) variables. See Table 5.1 for variable definitions.

Regression Analysis

We use the unbalanced panel regression model in this study but a question arises whether the fixed effect or random effect model is appropriate for our dataset. So, we conduct the Hausman (1978) test for the preferable model. This test results show that the fixed effect is more robust than random effect. Hence, we choose the fixed effects model to determine the capital structure of 72 water companies. Table 4 displays that the estimated coefficient of PROFIT does not impact on LEV and STD. These results support H_0. However, fixed effects regressions result shows that PROFIT is negatively associated with LTD at 10% level of significance. Thus, H_{1b} is supported and tends to suggest that pecking order theory holds in a significant manner for the 72 water companies studied. Our finding is consistent with Alipour et al. (2015) who report that PROFIT negatively correlated with LTD at 10% level. The negative coefficient for PROFIT indicates that profitable water companies require less external long-term loan financing. The estimated coefficient for water companies SIZE does not seem to impact LEV significantly. This result supports H_0. However, water companies SIZE is negatively and significantly linked with LTD at 10% level, whereas poses a positive relationship with STD in fixed effects regression. The result indicates that smaller water companies borrow short-term loan for external financing.

However, smaller water companies may have struggle for borrow LTD because information asymmetry is severe issue in small water companies. This finding is line with agency theory and as noted in the previous findings (Abor and Biekpe, 2009; Alipour et al., 2015; Vo, 2017). The estimated results show that AGE is positively related and significant with LEV and LTD (5% level). The estimated coefficients support hypothesis H_{3a}. The assumption holds that older water companies appear to have good credit history. So, older companies easily borrow debt without debt related agency issues (Abor and Biekpe, 2009; Frank and Goyal 2009). We find that RISK positively and significantly impacts on LEV and STD at 10% and 1% levels, respectively. This results support H_{4a} and are in line with Esperanca et al. (2003) and Chen (2004), respectively. These results suggest that the trade-off theory holds significantly also for the 72 water companies in this case. However,

RISK is not correlated with LTD so H_0 is accepted. The estimated coefficients show that the FCF is negatively related with LEV, STD, and LTD at 1% and 5 % levels respectively. These results support H_{5b} and suggests that the return from investment would be quite low for water companies because the investment is sub-optimal by finance manager or possibly involves self-interested behaviour as the water companies reserve abnormal FCF, instead of distributing cash dividend for extra cash to the shareholders to relieve the agency issues (Akhtar, 2017). The findings show that TANG is negatively and significantly correlated with STD at 1% level. This finding is support H_{6b} hypothesis and consistent with Abor and Biekpe (2009) and Fauzi et al. (2013). This result supports the Jensen and Meckling (1976) agency theory, as tangible assets reduce the agency costs of debts.

Table 4. The fixed effect regression results for the determinants of capital structure

Variable	Model 1 - LEV		Model 2 - LTD		Model 3 – STD	
	Coef.	P > t	Coef.	P > t	Coef.	P > t
PROFIT	0.000	0.971	-0.001	0.065*	-0.000	0.287
SIZE	-0.000	0.242	-5.705	0.077*	0.000	0.009***
AGE	0.710	0.043**	0.080	0.059**	-0.005	0.738
RISK	0.002	0.072*	0.000	0.532	0.000	0.002***
FCF	-0.000	0.007***	-2.705	0.066*	-2.905	0.005***
TANG	0.002	0.423	0.000	0.306	-0.000	0.017***
NDTS	-0.153	0.000***	-0.007	0.000***	0.000	0.038**
GROWTH	0.001	0.000***	0.000	0.000***	6.520	0.969
C	0.106	0.936	-0.096	0.536	0.082	0.167
R-squad	0.013	-	0.016	-	0.032	-

Notes: This table displays the results of unbalanced panel (fixed effects) regressions of Equations (5.1) and (5.2) to determine the capital structure of 72 private water companies. The dependent variables are capital structure (LEV, LTD and STD) and the independent variable includes performance, which is defined as the Stock Returns (RET). See Table 5.1 for variable definitions. p-values are given in parentheses.

*, ** and *** represent significance at 10, 5and 1% levels, respectively; and p-values are given in brackets.

Our finding indicates that water companies can borrow more short-term funds from financial institutions without collateral value if the companies have more TANG. It is important to note that higher TANG values may be used for smaller number of short-term funds, which would be a more adaptable for financial structure (Vo, 2017). The coefficients of NDTS measure are negatively correlated with LEV and LTD at 1% level. Hence, H_{7b} is accepted. Similar results are noted in Akhtar and Oliver (2009) and Ramli et al. (2019) - a negative relationship between NDTS and LEV. However, STD is positive and significant with NDTS at 5% level. This result supports H_{7a} and line with Fauzi et al. (2013). The coefficients of GROWTH measure are positively associated with LEV and LTD at 1% level. These results are line with Balios et al., (2016). However, the results show no significant relations with STD so H_0 is accepted.

CONCLUSION

In concluding, we note that the capital structure is measured by leverage, long-term debt and short-term debt (Reza, 2017). We empirically examine whether the determinants of capital structure of 72 water companies for the period of 2004-2014. We identifiy and use eight water companies' attributes variables (PROFIT, SIZE, AGE, RISK. FCF, TANG, NDTS and GROWTH) to help understand explain the capital structure. This study uses an unbalanced panel (fixed effect) regression model, where LEV, LTD and STD are assumed to a function of water companies' attributes - variables as hypothesized from the review of the capital structure theories literature. The fixed effect regression shows that PROFIT, FCF and TANG variables confirm the pecking-order theory in that these variables are negatively correlated with capital structure; whereas AGE, RISK and GROWTH relations support the trade-off theory because these variables are noted to be positively associated with capital structure. The SIZE and NDTS variables are positive and significantly related to STD. These two variables support the trade-off theory. However, SIZE and NDTS negatively impact on LTD. Thus, the pecking-order theory is accepted by water companies. Therefore, the results offer the different determinants of capital structure for LEV, LTD and STD of water companies. It is important to note that these results are consistent with expectations.

The findings of the study undoubtedly provide a framework for understanding the capital structure financing decision and thus critical for the world water companies as they use different funding sources. The findings also have an important theoretical and applied implication in terms of the two theories noted earlier. Further, our study also would be useful for most executives of water companies' who are keen to favour optimal capital structure in their attempt to increase the profitability and thus distribute more dividends to shareholders. Unfortunately, owing to data limitations, this study is used an unbalanced panel data and therefore it was not possible to examine the details for this negative outcome in further detail. It will be beneficial to repeat this research when balanced panel data becomes available. Moreover, the research can be further extended along with a balanced panel data to determine how extreme events influence capital structures – for example, the relationship between COVID-19 and capital structure to examine how COVID-19 influences water companies financing decision-making when in stress conditions exist.

REFERENCES

Abor, Joshua. & Nicholas Biekpe. (2009). "How do we explain the capital structure of SMEs in sub-Saharan Africa? Evidence from Ghana." *Journal of Economic Studies*, *36* (1), 83-97.

Akhtar, Shumi. & Barry Oliver. (2009). "Determinants of capital structure for Japanese multinational and domestic corporations." *International Review of Finance*, *9*, 1-26.

Akhtar, Shumi. (2005). "The determinants of capital structure for Australian multinational and domestic corporations." *Australian Journal of Management*, *30*, 321-341.

Akhtar, Shumi. (2017). "Capital structure of multinational and domestic corporations – a cross-country comparison." *Accounting and Finance*, *57*, 319-349.

Al-Ajmi, J., Hameeda Abo Hussain. & Nadhem Al-Saleh. (2009). "Decisions on capital structure in a Zakat environment with prohibition of Riba." *Journal of Risk Finance*, *10* (5), 460 - 476.

Al-Fayoumi, Nedal A. & Bana M. Abuzayed. (2009). "Ownership structure and corporate financing." *Applied Financial Economics*, *19* (24), 1975-1986.

Alipour, Mohammadi. & Mir Farhad Seddigh Mohammadi Hojjatollah Derakhshan. (2015). "Determinants of capital structure: an empirical study of firms in Iran." *International Journal of Law and Management*, *57*(1), 53-83.

Alvarez, Marta. & Javier Rodriguez. (2015). "Water-related mutual funds: Investment performance and social role." *Social Responsibility Journal*, *11*(3), 502-512.

Antoniou, A., Barr, D. G. & Priestley, R. (2000). "Abnormal stock returns and public policy: The case of the UK privatised electricity and water utilities." *Journal of Finance and Economics*, *5*(2), 93-107.

Antoniou, Antonios, Yilmaz Guney. & Krishna Paudya. (2008). "The determinants of capital structure: capital market-oriented versus bank-oriented institutions." *Journal of Financial and Quantitative Analysis*, *43* (1), 59-92.

Arvanitis, Stavros H., Irakleia S. Tzigkounaki, Theodoros V. Stamatopoulos. & Eleftherios I. Thalassinos. (2012). "Dynamic approach of capital structure of European shipping companies." *International Journal of Economic Sciences and Applied Research*, *5*(3), 33-63.

Baker, M. & Jeffrey Wurgler. (2002). "Market Timing and Capital Structure." *Journal of Finance*, *57*, 1-32.

Balios, D., Daskalakis, N., Eriotis, N. & Vasiliou, D. (2016). "SMEs capital structure determinants during severe economic crisis: The case of Greece." *Cogent Economics & Finance*, *4*, 1-11.

Berkman1, Ayberk Nuri Ömer İskenderoğlu, Erdinç Karadeniz. & Nazif Ayyildiz. (2016). "Determinants of Capital Structure: The Evidence from European Energy Companies." *International Journal of Business Administration*, *7*(6), 9-106.

Booth, Laurence, Varouj Aivazian, Asli Demirguc-Kunt. & Vojislav. (2001). "Capital structure in developing countries." *Journal of Finance*, *56* (1), 87-130.

Bryman, Alen. & Duncan Cramer. (1997). *Quantitative Data Analysis with SPSS for Windows: A Guide for Social Scientists*. Routledge. London.

Buckland, Roger, Janice Beecher. & Julian Williams. (2015). "Risk and regulation in water utilities: A cross-country comparison of evidence from the CAPM." *Journal of Regulatory Economics*, *47* (2), 117-145.

Buckland, Roger. & Patricia Fraser. (2001). "Political and regulatory risk in water utilities: Beat sensitivity in the United Kingdom." *Journal of Business Finance and Accounting*, (7-8), 877-904.

Cai, Jiannan, Shuai Li. & Hubo Cai. (2019). "Empirical Analysis of Capital Structure Determinants in Infrastructure Projects under Public–Private Partnerships." *Journal of Construction Engineering and Management*, *145* (5), 1-9.

Chakraborty, Indrani. (2010). "Capital structure in an emerging stock market-case of India." *Research in International Business and Finance*, *24* (3), 295-314.

Chen, Jean J. (2004). "Determinants of capital structure of Chinese listed companies." *Journal of Business Research*, *57* (12), 1341-1351.

Cortez, Michael Angelo. & Stevie Susanto. (2012). "The determinants of corporate capital structure: evidence from Japanese manufacturing companies." *Journal of International Business Research*, *11* (3), 122-134.

Dammon Robert. & Lemma W. Senbet. (1988). "The effect of taxes and depreciation on corporate investment and financial leverage." *Journal of Finance*, *43*, 3 - 29.

De Angelo, Harry. & Ronald W. Masulis. (1980). "Leverage and Dividend Irrelevancy Under Corporate and Personal Taxation." *Journal of Finance*, *35*, 453–517.

Ebaid, Ibrahim El-Sayed. (2009). "The impact of capital-structure choice on firm performance: Empirical evidence from Egypt." *Journal of Risk Finance*, *10*(5), 477-487.

Esperança, José Paulo, Ana Paula Matias Gama. & Mohamed Azzim Gulamhussen. (2003). "Corporate debt policy of small firms: an empirical (re)examination." *Journal of Small Business and Enterprise Development*, *10*, 62-80.

Fama, Eugene F. & Kenneth R. French. (2002). "Testing trade-off and pecking order predictions about dividends and debt." *Review of Financial Studies*, *15* (1), 1-33.

Fauzi, Fitriya, Abdul Basyith. & Muhammad Idris. (2013). "The Determinants of Capital Structure: An Empirical Study of New

Zealand-Listed Firms." *Asian Journal of Finance & Accounting*, *5*(2), 1-21.

Frank, Murray Z. & Goyal Vidhan. K. Goyal. (2003). "Testing the pecking order theory of capital structure." *Journal of Financial Economics*, *67* (2), 217-248.

Frank, Murray Z. & Goyal Vidhan. K. Goyal. (2009). "Capital structure decisions: which factors are reliably important?" *Financial Management*, *38* (1), 1-37.

Geman, Hélyette. & Alois Kanyinda. (2007). "Water as the next commodity." *The Journal of Alternative Investments*, *10* (2), 23-31.

Hall, Graham C., Patrick J. Hutchinson. & Nicos Michaelas. (2004). "Determinants of the capital structure of European SMEs." *Journal of Business Finance and Accounting*, *31*(5-6), 711-728.

Harris, Milton. & Artur Raviv. (1991). "The theory of capital structure." *Journal of Finance*, *46* (1), 297-355.

Hassan Omar Moalin. & Gurudeo Anand Tularam. (2018). "The effects of climate change on rural-Urban migration in Sub-Saharan Africa (SSA) - The Cases of Democratic Republic of Congo, Kenya and Niger." In *Applications in Water Systems Management and Modeling*, ed. Daniela Malcangio, 3-31. London: IntechOpen.

Jensen, Michael C. & William H. Meckling. (1976). "Theory of the firm: managerial behavior, agency costs and ownership structure." *Journal of Financial Economics*, *3*(4), 305-360.

Jin, Yizheng, Bin Li, Eduardo Roca. & Victor Wong. (2015). "Water as an investment: Liquid yet illiquid!" *Applied Economics*, *48*(9), 731-745.

Jin, Yizheng, Eduardo Roca, Bin Li, Eduardo Roca. & Wong, V. (2014). "Investment returns in the water industry: a survey." *Intonational Journal of Water*, *8*(2), 183 - 199.

Jin, Yizheng, Rajibur Reza, Li, B., Eduardo Roca. & Victor Wong. (2019). "Water as an investment and the impact of regulatory risk." *Financial Planning Research Journal*, *5*(1), 55-81.

Kaur, Raghvir. & Rao, N. Krishna. (2009). "Determinants of capital structure: experience of Indian cotton textile industry", *The XIMB Journal of Management*, *6* (2), 97-112.

Kavita Sachwani. (2020). *Financing the water sector – An alternate approach.* Available at: https://www.2030wrg.org/financing-the-water-sector-an-alternate-approach/#_ftnref1.

Kester, W. Carl. (1986). "Capital and ownership structure: a comparison of United States and Japanese manufacturing corporations." *Financial Management*, *15*, 5-16.

Kraus, Alan. & Robert H. Litzenberger. (1973). "A State-Preference Model of Optimal Financial Leverage." *Journal of Finance*, *28*(4), 911-922.

Mateeva, Miroslav, Panikkos Poutziouris, P. & Konstantin Ivanov. (2013). "On the determinants of SME capital structure of Eastern and Central Europe – a dynamic panel analysis", *Research in International Business and Finance*, *27* (1), 28-51.

Mekonnen, Mesfin M. & Arjen Y. Hoekstra. (2016). 'Four Billion People Facing Severe Water Scarcity.' *Science Advances*, *2*, 1-6.

Michaelas, Nicos, Francis Chittenden. & Panikkos Poutziouris. (1999). "Financial policy and capital structure choice in UK SMEs: empirical evidence from company panel Data", *Small Business Economics*, *12* (2), 113-130.

Modigliani, Franco, and Metron H. Miller. 1958. "The cost of capital, corporation finance and the Theory of Investment." *American Economic Review*, *48* (3), 261-297.

Modigliani, Franco. & Metron H. Miller. (1963). "Corporate income taxes and the cost of capital: a correction." *American Economic Review*, *53* (3), 433-443.

Morana, Claudio. & John W. Sawkins. (2000). "Regulatory uncertainty and share price volatility: The English and Welsh water industry's periodic price review." *Journal of Regulatory Economics*, *17*, 87-100.

Myers, Stewart. C. & Nichilas S. Majluf. (1984). "Corporate financing and investment decision when firms have information investors do not have", *Journal of Financial Economics*, *13* (2), 187-221.

Myers, Stewart. C. (1977). "Determinants of corporate borrowing", *Journal of Financial Economics*, *5* (2), 147-175.

Myers, Stewart. C. (1984). "The capital structure puzzle", *Journal of Finance*, Vol. *39* (3), 574-592.

Nguyen, Tran Dinh Khoi. & Neelakantan Ramachandran. (2006). "Capital structure in small and medium sized enterprises: the case of Vietnam." *ASEAN Economic Bulletin*, *23*(2), 192-211.

Orlovaa, Svetlana, Joel T. Harperb. & Li Suna. (2020). "Determinants of capital structure complexity." *Journal of Economics and Business* 110: 1-19.

Pescetto, Gioia. M. (2008). "Regulation and systematic risk: The case of the water industry in England and Wales." *Applied Financial Economics*, *181*, 61-73.

Phooi M'ng, Jacinta Chan, Mahfuzur Rahman. & Selvam Sannacy. (2017). "The determinants of capital structure: Evidence from public listed companies in Malaysia, Singapore and Thailand." *Cogent Economics & Finance*, *5*, 1-34.

Piñeiro-Chousaa, Juan., M. Ángeles López-Cabarcos. & Domingo Ribeiro-Soriano. (2020). "Does investor attention influence water companies' stock returns?" *Technology Forecasting & Social Change*, *158*, 1-10.

Rajan, Raghuram G. & Luigi Zingales. (1995). "What do we know about capital structure? Some evidence from international data." *Journal of Finance*, *50* (5), 1421-1460.

Ramli, Nur Ainna, Hengky Latanb. & Grace T. Solovida. (2019). "Determinants of capital structure and firm financial performance—A PLS-SEM approach: Evidence from Malaysia and Indonesia." *The Quarterly Review of Economics and Finance*, *71*, 148 -160.

Reza, Rajibur. & Gurudeo Anand Tularam. (2017). An analysis of the relationships between ownership structure and capital structure of the global water industry. *22nd International Congress on Modelling and Simulation*, Hobart, Tasmania, Australia, 188-194.

Reza, Rajibur. (2017). An investigation of water investment performance: Analysis of the global water industry. *PhD Thesis*. Griffith University, Australia. Available at: https://research-repository.griffith.edu.au/handle/10072/371256.

Reza, Rajibur., Gurudeo Anand Tularam. & Bin Li. (2017). "An investigation into the interdependence of global water indices: a VAR analysis." *Applied Economics*, *49*, 769-796.

Reza, Rajibur., Gurudeo Anand Tularam. & Bin Li. (2018). "Returns and volatility of water investments." *Cogent Economics and. Finance*, *6*, 1-33.

Roca, Eduardo. & Gurudeo Anand Tularam. (2012). "Which way does water flow? An econometric analysis of the global price integration of water stocks." *Applied Economics*, *44*(23), 2935-2944.

Roca, Eduardo., Gurudeo Anand Tularam. & Rajibur Reza. (2015). "Fundamental signals of investment profitability in the global water industry." *International Journal of Water*, *9*, 395-424.

Sangeetha, M. & Sivathaasan, N. (2013). Factors Determining Capital Structure: A Case study of listed companies in Sri Lanka. *Research Journal of Finance and Accounting*, *4*(6), 236-247.

Shyam-Sunder, Lakshmi. & Stewart. C. Myers. (1999). "Testing static tradeoff against pecking order models of capital structure." *Journal of Financial Economics*, *51* (2), 219-244.

Sikveland, Marius. & Dengjun Zhang. (2020). "Determinants of capital structure in the Norwegian salmon aquaculture industry." *Marine Policy*, *119*, 1-7.

Sogorb-Mira, Francisco. (2005). "How SME uniqueness affects capital structure evidence from 1994-1998 Spanish data panel." *Small Business Economics*, *25* (5), 447-457.

Titman, Sheridan. & Roberto Wessels. (1988). "The determinants of capital structure choice." *Journal of Finance*, *43*(1), 1-19.

Tularam, Gurudeo Anand. & Mahbub Illahee. (2010). "Time series analysis of rainfall and temperature interactions in coastal catchments." *Journal of Mathematics and Statistics*, *6*(3), 372-380.

Tularam, Gurudeo Anand. & Omar Moalin Hassan (2015). "Water availability and food security: Implication of people's movement and migration in sub-Saharan Africa (SSA)." In: *Groundwater Assessment, Modeling, and Management*, ed. M. Thangarajan and Vijay P. Singh, 405-426.New York: CRC Press.

Tularam, Gurudeo Anand. & Omar Moalin Hassan. (2016). "The vulnerable nature of water security in Sub-Saharan Africa (SSA) - A country by country analysis." In: *Handbook on Africa: Challenges and Issues of the 21st century*, ed. Whitney Sherman, 47-83. Hauppauge/New York: Nova Science Publishers.

Tularam, Gurudeo Anand. & Rajibur Reza. (2016). "Water exchange traded funds: A study on idiosyncratic risk using Markov switching analysis." *Cogent Economics and. Finance*, *4*(1), 1-12.

Tularam, Gurudeo Anand. & Rajibur Reza. (2017). "The critical importance of groundwater in coastal areas: Impact of climate change on Bangladesh freshwater resources." *Journal of Climate Change*, *3*, 59-70.

Vandone, Daniela, Lucia Bald. & Alessandra Tanda. (2018). "The impact of energy and agriculture prices on the stock performance of the water industry." *Water Resource and Economics*, *23*, 1-14.

Vo, Xuan Vinh. (2017). "Determinants of capital structure in emerging markets: Evidence from Vietnam." *Research in International Business and Finance*, *40*, 105-113.

Zhang, Ye. (2010). "The product category effects on capital structure: evidence from the SMEs of British manufacturing industry." *International Journal of Business and Management*, Vol. *5*(8), 86-113.

In: Advances in Capital Structure Research ISBN: 978-1-53619-948-2
Editor: Karel Marleau

Chapter 2

CAPITAL STRUCTURE AND MACROECONOMIC CONDITIONS: A REVIEW OF THE LITERATURE AND A RESEARCH AGENDA

Antonio D'Amato*
Department of Economic & Statistics,
University of Salerno, Fisciano, SA, Italy

ABSTRACT

Research on firm capital structure and macroeconomic conditions has gained momentum in recent years, particularly following the 2007-2008 global financial crisis. Similarly, the recent macroeconomic downturn due to the COVID-19 pandemic and the subsequent corporate liquidity problems highlight the importance of a comprehensive analysis of corporate financing issues under different macroeconomic conditions. However, what do we know about the relationship between firm capital structure and macroeconomic events? This chapter aims to answer this question via a systematic literature review (SLR) to highlight the key contributors, the key areas of investigation and the main results in

* Corresponding Author's E-mail: andamato@unisa.it.

the literature and to ultimately suggest a future research agenda for the field.

Based on a comprehensive sample of 156 articles published from 1992 to 2020 and retrieved from the Web of Science (WoS) database, we apply an SLR and a bibliometric analysis to investigate the main characteristics of the literature on the relationship between firm capital structure and different macroeconomic states. Specifically, we highlight the evolution of this path of research over the years and the most influential authors, types of publications, and journals. Moreover, we identify the main research areas in the field. The first area of research focuses on the adjustment of the debt/equity level under different macroeconomic conditions. The determinants of firm capital structure in different macroeconomic states represent the second area of research. The main research gaps and the future research agenda are also discussed.

Keywords: capital structure, macroeconomic conditions, crisis, systematic literature review

INTRODUCTION

The capital structure is a cornerstone of modern corporate finance theory due to its impacts on firm competitiveness, governance and performance. In particular, the capital structure is an important decision for firms because it affects the cost of capital; hence, it can lead to the maximization of firm value. In this respect, there is a large body of literature on the capital structure with a long history starting with the seminal works of Lintner (1956), Hirshleifer (1958) and Modigliani and Miller (1958). Although the capital structure literature has taken different directions, the majority of studies in the field mainly investigate firm-level factors (e.g., profitability, risk, growth opportunities) that affect the mix between equity and debt (Frank and Goyal 2009; Titman and Wessels 1988). Research at the cross-country level has shown that capital structure decisions are impacted not only by firm characteristics but also by institutional and macroeconomic variables (Beck, Demirgüç-Kunt, and Maksimovic 2008; de Jong, Kabir, and Nguyen 2008; Rajan and Zingales 1995; Antoniou, Guney, and Paudyal 2008). However, despite the substantial literature that has developed in the capital structure field, it is surprising that little attention has been paid to the impact of macroeconomic conditions on the capital structure of firms. Specifically, in the early 2000s, research on the capital structure and macroeconomic states began to increase, and in recent years, it has gained momentum, particularly following the 2007-2008 global financial crisis. Similarly, the recent macroeconomic downturn due to the COVID-19 pandemic and the subsequent liquidity problems of firms highlight the importance of investigating how corporate financing decision making operates in different macroeconomic states (Halling, Yu, and Zechner 2020; Ellul, Erel, and Rajan 2020). It is well known that the economic cycle affects business growth opportunities and default risk, which in turn affect the availability of external funds and their costs (Yeh and Roca 2012). Therefore, understanding the role of macroeconomic factors in capital structure decisions is fundamental at both the macro and firms levels, confirming the need to explore this topic in more detail.

With the aim of contributing to the field, in this chapter, we conduct a comprehensive review and critical analysis of the literature to highlight the knowledge structure of the topic of our interest and suggest a future research agenda.

Based on 156 papers published between 1992 and 2020 and retrieved from the Web of Science (WoS) database, we first analyze the general characteristics of the literature (e.g., types of studies, languages, areas of study) on the relationship between macroeconomic conditions and capital structure decisions. Second, we create a citation map of the sampled publications and identify the citation relationships and, consequently, the research fields on the topic. In this respect, we identify two main research areas. The first concerns the adjustment of the debt/equity level under different macroeconomic conditions. The second has to do with the determinants of firm capital structure in different macroeconomic states. Finally, we highlight potential future research directions to expand the knowledge on the topic.

The remainder of this chapter is organized as follows. In the next section, we present the methodology used in this study. Then, we present the descriptive results and the bibliometric analysis of the literature. Finally, we discuss future research directions.

METHODS

As stated above, the aim of this chapter is to perform a comprehensive literature review using an SLR approach to examine, on the one hand, the general characteristics of the literature on firm capital structure and macroeconomic conditions. On the other hand, we aim to map the field of research to highlight the dominant streams of research and to then identify gaps in the literature and propose future research directions.

The SLR method has a well-established history and is used in different areas of research, from medicine to management, to map the evolution of the literature in a given field of research (Tranfield, Denyer, and Smart 2003; Kraus, Breier, and Dasí-Rodríguez 2020). Specifically, this method is a process composed of three steps. In the first step, the researcher selects the database (e.g., WoS, Scopus) from which to collect papers, and he or she identifies the most suitable set of keywords to find the most relevant papers in the field of research. In the second step, the most relevant works are identified via a set of selection criteria (e.g., languages, types of publications, fields of research). Finally, the papers are analyzed, and the results are presented and discussed.

In this study, we used HistCite™, one of the most well-known software packages for bibliometric analysis. It provides tools for descriptive and citation analysis.

Regarding the first step, in this study, we used the WoS database to investigate the literature on the topic of interest. The WoS database is one of the most popular scientific databases, enjoying remarkable prestige in the academic world. It is a bibliographic and citation database that allows research in over 12,000 journals and 148,000 conference proceedings in the sciences, social sciences, arts and humanities.

In the WoS database, to identify relevant studies investigating the relationship between firm capital structure and macroeconomic conditions, we defined a set of appropriate keywords. For this purpose, we analyzed a series of articles among the most influential in the field to identify the most suitable keywords that could define the topic. Therefore, we defined two search strings for the two core concepts of our research, namely, "capital structure" and "macroeconomic conditions".

Thus, the first string is defined as follows: ("Capital structure" OR "Financial structure" OR "Debt financing" OR "Equity financing" OR "Financial leverage" OR "Financ* decision*"). The second string is as follows: (Crisis OR Crises OR "Macroeconomic condition*" OR "Macroeconomic state*" OR Recession OR Expansion OR Turmoil OR Pandemic OR Epidem* OR Disaster). Therefore, we collected all the publications included in the WoS database that included the keywords we defined in the title, among the author keywords or in the abstract. The search was run on the WoS database in March 2021, and we initially retrieved 766 papers published through 31 December 2020. The publications available since 2021 (12 documents) were excluded. From this initial set, we excluded papers not pertaining to the fields of economics, business finance, management and business. Following these exclusion/inclusion criteria, we obtained a final set of 602 articles. To include only those papers in line with the field of interest, we analyzed the abstracts of the sampled articles and excluded those papers that covered a topic not in line with our purpose. In particular, we also excluded articles that dealt with the impact of macroeconomic conditions on banking and/or the financial industry.

Based on these selection criteria, we obtained a final sample of 156 papers published from 1992 to 2020 that were suitable for our analysis.

From the WoS database, we retrieved the following information for each paper: the name(s) of the author(s), the title, the name of the journal, citation details (the volume, issue and page numbers), the abstract and keywords, the language of the paper, the type of publication (e.g., journal article, conference proceeding), the country of origin of the authors and the institutional affiliation of the authors. Furthermore, we obtained a full record of the cited references (i.e., the references cited by each sampled paper) and the number of times each document was cited. The downloaded data were used to investigate the general characteristics of the literature in the research field and to produce the bibliographic map described in the next section. We manually checked the citation records to manage inconsistencies as needed.

DESCRIPTIVE RESULTS AND BIBLIOMETRIC ANALYSIS

In this section, we present the results of the descriptive and bibliometric analysis of the 156 papers retrieved from the WoS database. In particular, the publications are analyzed in terms of the time trend, publication types, languages, the journals where the articles were published and countries and institutions where the authors are based.

Regarding the time trend of the papers (Figure 1), we highlight that this topic is a fairly recent research area. Only nine out of the 156 papers (approximately 6%) collected in the WoS database and investigating the impact of macroeconomic conditions on firm capital structure were published before the global financial crisis, with the first paper dating back to 1992. After the 2007-2008 global financial crisis and the subsequent sovereign debt crisis of 2012, there was growing interest in the topic. This increased interest is probably attributable to a perceived greater frequency of crisis events in the future due to the growing globalization of economies and, consequently, the greater risks of systemic crises. Clearly, following the crisis triggered by the recent COVID-19 pandemic, which has caused a global recession with a negative impact on firms' financial conditions, we think that interest in the field could further grow.

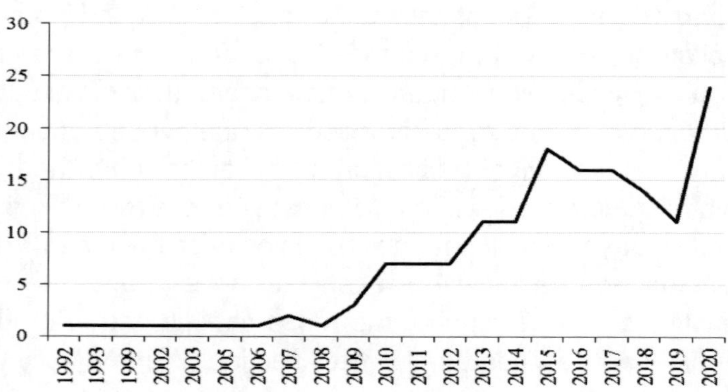

Figure 1. Time trend of published articles on the capital structure and macroeconomic conditions.

Table 1. Type of source

Type of publication	No.	%
Journal article	121	77.5%
Conference proceeding	28	18.0%
Book chapter	7	4.5%
Total	156	100%

Regarding the characteristics of the publications, Table 1 classifies the sampled papers by publication type. Approximately 77.6% (121 out of 156) are articles published in scientific journals, of which 6.78% are forthcoming articles, 18% (28 out of 156) are conference proceedings, and the remainder are book chapters.

Almost all of the sampled papers were written in English, and the presence of papers written in other languages is negligible.

In regard to the journals engaged in disseminating content in line with our topic of interest, we found 81 journals that published the articles (121) included in our sample. Of these journals, 51 are peer-reviewed journals with an impact factor (63%), and 26 journals published at least 2 papers on the subject. A total of 67% of the journals have made one contribution to this area. More interestingly, 50% of the journals that have published in this area have an impact factor greater than 2, which indicates that the topic is of interest to the top-rated journals. Specifically, these journals published approximately 30% of all the sampled articles. Finally, 19 (15.7%) articles were published in journals classified as 4 or 4 * by the Academic Journal Guide (AJG) 2018. Table 2 shows the top 13 most active journals in the field. The Journal of Corporate Finance, which is a leading journal in the field of corporate finance, is the top contributor, with 6 articles. The top 13 journals published 45 articles, equal to 28.8% of all the sampled papers.

Table 3 presents the top ten contributing institutions. This analysis is performed starting with the analysis of the affiliation of the authors of the collected papers. First, the number of universities/institutions with which authors are affiliated is 248. However, most of these institutions contributed to the debate in the research field with a single article. Only 16% of them contributed 2 or more articles. City University of Hong Kong contributed 4 articles. In addition to City University of Hong Kong,

Bocconi University and the Center for Economic Policy Research (CEPR) are among the top contributing universities.

Regarding the countries contributing to the scientific debate on the topic, a total of 47 countries are represented in our sample. The United States is the country with the most contributions, 35 papers (22.4%), followed by the UK, with 23 papers (14.7%), and China, with 16 papers (10.26%). These top three countries contribute nearly 50% of all the documents analyzed in this study, and this ranking confirms that the United States and the UK are the leading countries in research on financial topics.

Table 2. Top contributing journals

No.	Journal	Publisher	JIF	AJG	Papers	%
1.	*Journal of Corporate Finance*	Elsevier	2.521	4	6	3.8
2.	*International Review of Financial Analysis*	Elsevier	2.497	3	4	2.6
3.	*Journal of Financial Economics*	Elsevier	5.731	4*	4	2.6
4.	*Research in International Business and Finance*	Elsevier	1.801	2	4	2.6
5.	*Small Business Economics*	Springer Nature	4.803	3	4	2.6
6.	*Emerging Markets Finance and Trade*	Taylor & Francis	1.214	2	3	1.9
7.	*Journal of Economic Studies*	Emerald	n.a.		3	1.9
8.	*Journal of Property Investment & Finance*	Emerald	n.a.	1	3	1.9
9.	*Post-Communist Economies*	Taylor & Francis	0.875	1	3	1.9
10.	*Quarterly Review of Economics and Finance*	Elsevier	n.a.	2	3	1.9
11.	*Review of Financial Studies*	Oxford UP	4.649	4*	3	1.9
12.	*Tourism Economics*	SAGE	1.819	2	3	1.9
13.	*Applied Economics*	Taylor & Francis	1.103	2	2	1.3

Table 3. Top ten contributing institutions

No.	Institution	No. of papers
1.	City University Hong Kong	4
2.	Bocconi University	3
3.	Center for Economic Policy Research (CEPR)	3
4.	Mid Sweden University	3
5.	National Pingtung University of Science and Technology	3
6.	University of California, Berkeley	3
7.	University of Southampton	3
8.	American University of Sharjah	2
9.	Bangor University	2
10.	Banking University of Ho Chi Minh City	2

Table 4. Top seven contributing countries

No.	Country	No. of papers
1.	USA	35
2.	UK	23
3.	People's Republic of China	16
4.	Canada	11
5.	Italy	8
6.	Australia	6
7.	Greece	6

However, China is becoming one of the most important contributors in the scientific debate and not only in the field of financial studies. Regarding geographical areas, over half of the studies (58%) come from European countries, followed by countries in North America (29.5%) and Asia. Latin American countries are absent. Figure 2 shows the distribution of authors by their country of origin. This distribution is in line with the previous results regarding the geographical distribution of the collected papers.

Tables 5 and 6 present the most active authors and the top coauthors on the topic, respectively. A total of 327 scholars authored the sampled papers. Of these authors, 13.8% produced papers as single authors.

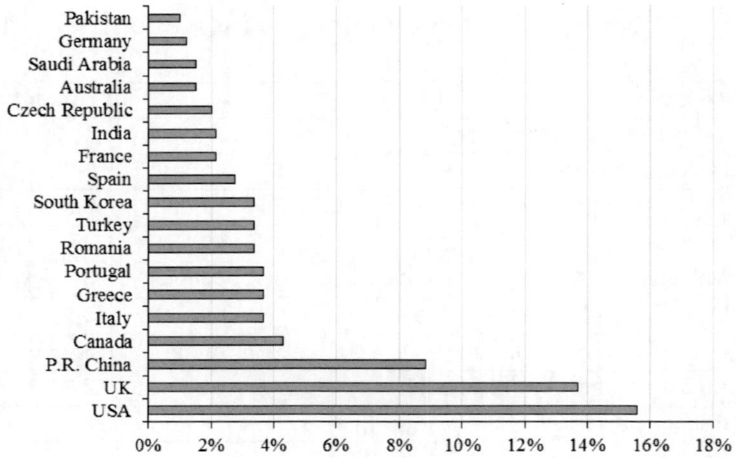

Figure 2. Distribution of researchers across countries.

Table 5. Top ten contributing authors

No.	Author	Institutional affiliation	Country	No. of papers
1.	Muncef Guizani	Prince Sattam Bin Abdulaziz University	Saudi Arabia	3
2.	Peter Ohman	Mid Sweden University	Sweden	3
3.	Zélia S. Serrasqueiro	University of Beira Interior	Portugal	3
4.	Darush Yazdanfar	Mid Sweden University	Sweden	3
5.	Dimitrios Balios	University of Athens	Greece	2
6.	Harjoat S. Bhamra	University of British Columbia	Canada	2
7.	Narjess Boubakri	American University of Sharjah	United Arab Emirates	2
8.	Saurabh Chadha	Indian Institute of Technology	India	2
9.	Hui Chen	MIT, Sloan School of Management	USA	2
10.	Jacinto V. da Silva	University of Évora	Portugal	2

Table 6. Top coauthors and joint publications

No.	Author 1	Author 2	Joint publications
1.	Peter Ohman	Darush Yazdanfar	3
2.	Dimitrios Balios	Nikolaus Daskalakis	2
3.	Harjoat S. Bhamra	Lars-Alexander Kuehn	2
4.	Harjoat S. Bhamra	Ilya A. Strebulaev	2

Therefore, most of the work is carried out in research teams consisting of at least two authors. Regarding the pairs of authors who have made the greatest contributions to research on the impact of macroeconomic conditions on firm capital structure, we found only four pairs of authors who have produced 2 or more papers.

The results obtained thus far show that the theme of the relationship between macroeconomic conditions and firm capital structure represents a young field of research that is still not well established. Despite the large number of works on the capital structure, the number of papers produced in our field of interest is still small. In addition, there are few well-established groups of scholars with a large number of papers. Therefore, this finding suggests the existence of further research opportunities along different directions.

Table 7 presents the distribution of sampled papers by the number of citations. Moreover, the table reports the proportion of papers in each range of citations and the minimum and maximum values of each range of citations. The number of citations is a signal of the quality of a paper. The results in Table 7 show that 70% of the papers in WoS are cited at least once. Notably, only six papers (3.8%) have more than one hundred citations. Regarding the range of citations, the range of 1-10 citations is the greatest, accounting for more than 46% of the papers.

In Table 8, we present the top contributing journals in the field, the number of papers published in each journal, which is a measure of productivity, and the number of citations of these papers, which is a measure of scientific influence on the academic community (Svensson 2010). Specifically, in Table 8, we show the global citations, the global citations per year and the average citations per paper. Although the Journal of Corporate Finance is the top contributor in the field, with six articles, it is not the most cited journal. The Journal of Financial

Economics is the most influential journal in the field, with 578 global citations and the highest number of citations per article (144.5) and per year (33.40), followed by Small Business Economics and the Review of Financial Studies.

Table 7. Distribution of papers by the number of citations

Citations	No. of papers	%	Min	Max
More than 100	6	3.8	105	304
51-100	4	2.6	59	97
31-50	8	5.1	32	50
21-30	8	5.1	21	30
11-20	11	7	11	20
1-10	72	46.1	1	10
0	47	30.1	0	

Table 8. Most frequently cited journals

No.	Journals	Articles	GC	GC/t	CA
1.	*Journal of Corporate Finance*	6	196	22.22	32.67
2.	*International Review of Financial Analysis*	4	103	11.71	25.75
3.	*Journal of Financial Economics*	4	578	33.40	144.5
4.	*Research in International Business and Finance*	4	7	2.33	1.75
5.	*Small Business Economics*	4	310	16.40	77.50
6.	*Emerging Markets Finance and Trade*	3	14	2.17	4.67
7.	*Journal of Economic Studies*	3	6	2.50	2.00
8.	*Journal of Property Investment & Finance*	3	5	0.90	1.67
9.	*Post-Communist Economies*	3	12	1.90	4.00
10.	*Quarterly Review of Economics and Finance*	3	37	6.39	12.33
11.	*Review of Financial Studies*	3	224	19.65	74.67
12.	*Tourism Economics*	3	19	3.12	6.33
13.	*Applied Economics*	2	2	0.67	1.00

GC global citations; GC/t global citations per year; CA citations per article

Regarding the most influential papers published in the field, we analyzed the global citations of each paper in our sample; these citations were retrieved from Clarivate Analytics–WoS. Citations are a measure of the impact of a given paper on the academic community, that is, its influence on other scholars. Therefore, in Table 9, we report the top ten most frequently cited papers, the publication and the classification of the journal where the paper was published according to the AJG 2018. Notably, the results reveal that the most frequently cited papers were published in high-impact journals rated 4* or 4. In particular, 70% of the articles presented in Table 9 appeared in 4*-rated journals.

Table 9. Top ten articles in the field by global citations

No.	Authors (year)	Journal	AJG(2018)	GC
1.	Korajczyk and Levy (2003)	*Journal of Financial Economics*	4*	304
2.	Choe, Masulis, and Nanda (1993)	*Journal of Empirical Finance*	3	294
3.	Michaelas, Chittenden, and Poutziouris (1999)	*Small Business Economics*	3	291
4.	Hackbarth, Miao, and Morellec (2006)	*Journal of Financial Economics*	4*	191
5.	Chen (2010)	*Journal of Finance*	4*	169
6.	Cook and Tang (2010)	*Journal of Corporate Finance*	4	105
7.	Bhamra HS, Kuehn LA, Strebulaev (2010a)	*Review of Financial Studies*	4*	97
8.	Bhamra HS, Kuehn LA, Strebulaev (2010b)	*Review of Financial Studies*	4*	68
9.	Dittmar and Dittmar (2008)	*Journal of Financial Economics*	4*	61
10.	Erel et al. (2012)	*Review of Financial Studies*	4*	59

In Table 10, we present the 7 most frequently cocited documents in our sample of articles. In cocitation, two given papers are present in the reference list of a single document. Therefore, cocitation is a means of discovering the similarity of a group of documents that deal with a similar subject area (Small 1973; Ferreira 2018). This analysis was performed using BibExcel, and we found that the most cocited works are Myers and Majluf (1984) and Rajan and Zingales (1995), which are cited together 39 times, followed by Jensen and Meckling (1976) and Myers and Majluf (1984). Together with Myers and Majluf (1984), the seminal work of Modigliani and Miller (1958) is only the seventh most frequently cited paper. Undoubtedly, the cocitation analysis shows that the works in our sample all pertain to the field of firm capital structure, which is a central theme of modern corporate finance.

RESULTS OF THE BIBLIOGRAPHIC MAPPING

To map the intellectual structure of our research field, we used bibliographic mapping, which is a well-established technique in the process of bibliometric analysis (Börner, Chen, and Boyack 2005). This technique allows us to visualize a bibliographic map, that is, the structure of a research field in terms of the most influential publications and the relationships between them. Consequently, scholars have the opportunity to identify the key research areas in the field, as well as the areas in which scholars are currently working and their evolution. This analysis is of great interest to academics who will be able to better target their research efforts towards those areas that are more promising or less investigated. Similarly, managers could also benefit from this analysis because it provides a clear idea of the state of knowledge in a given field of research so that it translates into business practices.

In this work, we mapped the literature using HistCite™ software (Linnenluecke 2017). Figure 3 illustrates the most locally cited publications within our sample of documents. To build the map, we used the local citation score (LCS), that is, the count of how many times a paper included in a given group of documents is cited by the remaining papers included in the same set. Of our 156 documents included in the initial set, 37 documents are cited locally at least once. Of these documents, 8 were eliminated because they have only one local citation and are included in a single relationship disconnected from a more structured network of documents.

Table 10. Top seven cocited documents in the sampled papers

No.	Papers	No. of cocitations
1.	Myers and Majluf (1984) - Rajan and Zingales (1995)	39
2.	Jensen and Meckling (1976) - Myers and Majluf (1984)	37
3.	Jensen and Meckling (1976) - Myers (1977)	34
4.	Myers (1984) - Myers and Majluf (1984)	34
5.	Jensen and Meckling (1976) - Rajan and Zingales (1995)	33
6.	Rajan and Zingales (1995) - Titman and Wessels (1988)	30
7.	Modigliani and Miller (1958) - Myers and Majluf (1984)	29

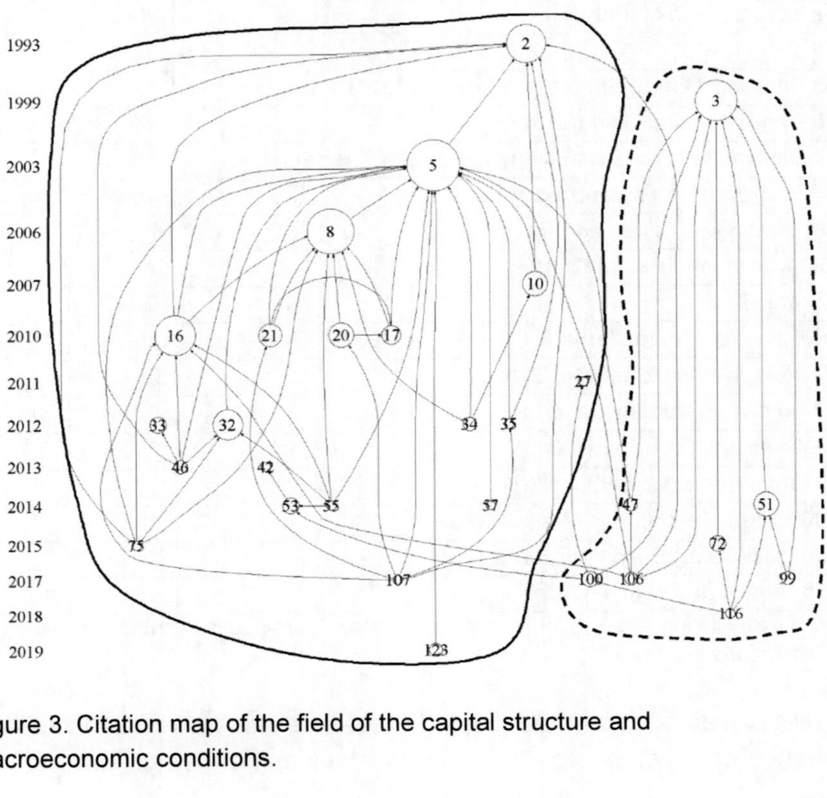

Figure 3. Citation map of the field of the capital structure and macroeconomic conditions.

Table 11. Highly locally cited papers in the citation network

Cluster 1	**GCS**	**LCS**
2 Choe, Masulis, and Nanda (1993)	294	16
5 Korajczyk and Levy (2003)	307	28
8 Hackbarth, Miao and Morellec (2006)	191	23
10 Levy and Hennessy (2007)	50	7
16 Cook and Tang (2010)	105	17
17 Bhamra, Kuehn and Strebulaev (2010b)	68	6
20 Chen (2010)	169	7
21 Bhamra, Kuehn and Strebulaev (2010a)	97	4
27 Voutsinas and Werner (2011)	22	1
32 Erel, Julio, Kim and Weisbach (2012)	59	10
33 Devos et al. (2012)	37	3
34 Yeh and Roca (2012)	10	2
35 Akhtar (2012)	13	1
42 Ebrahim and Mathur (2013)	2	1
46 Dang (2013)	30	2
53 Ebrahim, Girma, Shah and Williams (2014)	27	3
55 Dang, Kim and Shin (2014)	24	1
57 Dissanaike, Faasse, and Jayasekera (2014)	5	1
75 Drobetz, Schilling and Schroder (2015)	25	1
107 Baum, Caglayan, and Rashid (2017)	7	1
123 Moradi and Paulet (2019)	7	2
Cluster 2	**GCS**	**LCS**
3 Michaelas, Chittenden and Poutziouris (1999)	291	19
47 Mokhova and Zinecker (2014)	21	2
51 Proença, Laureano, and Laureano (2014)	19	7
72 Alves and Francisco (2015)	20	3
99 Öhman and Yazdanfar (2017)	7	2
100 Zeitun, Temimi and Mimouni (2017)	16	3
106 Daskalakis, Balios and Dalla (2017)	18	2
116 Van Hoang et al. (2018)	3	1

GCS global citation score; LCS local citation score. Each paper is numbered based on the nodes in Figure 3.

Moreover, based on an inspection of these single relationships, no evidence of new research areas in the development stage were found.

Therefore, the map we created is composed of 29 documents (see the list in Table 11). This low number of papers allows us to focus on the main, truly influential documents in the field of interest and, at the same time, to ensure that the map maintains high visual clarity, given the density of nodes and the connections between them. However, by using the entire dataset of documents, a more complex map of the literature in terms of nodes and connections is created, but it presents the same structure as that presented in Figure 3. Notably, a large number of documents in our dataset have little or no influence on the scientific debate in our field of research.

In Figure 3, documents are depicted as nodes (or circles), and the arrows represent the connections (citations) between them. The size of each node highlights the importance of the document in terms of the number of local citations that it has received from other papers within the dataset. Although the map does not present the entire dataset of available documents, it nevertheless makes it possible to identify the main research streams in the field. In Table 11, we present the list of documents mapped in Figure 3, which are divided into two research clusters identified based on the visual connections between the documents.

The first research cluster that we identified in our database is composed of works that mainly aim to formulate models that explain and predict the financial behavior of firms under different macroeconomic states.

The oldest paper that we identified in this cluster and that constitutes its cornerstone is that by Choe, Masulis, and Nanda (1993). They find evidence that firms issue new equity when they face lower adverse selection costs, which occurs during economic expansions. Korajczyk and Levy (2003) find that macroeconomic conditions impact financing decisions for unconstrained firms but do so to a lesser extent for constrained firms. Specifically, for the former, target leverage is countercyclical, while for the latter, it is procyclical. Therefore, compared to constrained firms, unconstrained firms time their issue choice to coincide with periods of favorable macroeconomic conditions. Furthermore, Hackbarth, Miao, and Morellec (2006) develop a framework for analyzing the impact of macroeconomic conditions on credit risk and dynamic capital structure choice via a contingent claims model of the leveraged firm, where the cash flow from operations depends on the state of the economy.

However, in this cluster, we recognized two main lines of research. The first line of research aims to explain the level of debt under different macroeconomic conditions by formulating theoretical models and conducting subsequent empirical tests. Using the predictions of agency theory regarding the effect of debt on the behavior of managers, Levy and Hennessy (2007) present a computable general equilibrium model explaining financing over the business cycle. They find that firms with less financing constraints exhibit pronounced countercylicality in leverage (Korajczyk and Levy 2003). Bhamra, Kuehn, and Strebulaev (2010a) and Bhamra, Kuehn, and Strebulaev (2010b) present a structural equilibrium framework, and consistent with previous empirical evidence, they find that the capital structure is procyclical at dates when firms releverage and that it is countercyclical in aggregate dynamics. Moreover, financially constrained firms choose more procyclical financing policies. Finally, Yeh and Roca (2012) present some empirical evidence from Taiwan's petrochemical, textile, and electronics industries during the period 1983-2007 and highlight that the debt ratios of firms are procyclical during the period before the 1997-98 Asian financial crisis but countercyclical during the period after this crisis.

The second line of research in this first cluster investigates the speed of adjustment of the capital structure to changes in macroeconomic conditions, and it originates with the work of Cook and Tang (2010). This line of research grew rapidly after the 2007-2008 global financial crisis and is predominantly empirical in nature. The main result that emerges in this stream of research is that firms adjust towards target leverage faster in good than in bad macroeconomic states (Drobetz, Schilling, and Schröder 2015). Therefore, in severe recessions, movement towards target leverage ratios is impeded by poor economic conditions. In the same line, Dang, Kim, and Shin (2014) document a negative impact of the global financial crisis on the speed of leverage adjustment. In particular, firms adjust their capital structures more quickly in a good macroeconomic state. However, this effect depends on the financial constraints that firms have to deal with.

Interestingly, Ebrahim et al. (2014) investigate the effect of political patronage on firm capital structure. They find that during a crisis,

Malaysian firms amend their capital structures. Moreover, politically patronized firms deleverage quicker than unconnected firms. Therefore, politically connected firms suffer in crisis periods because the government's ability to provide subsidies is reduced (Johnson and Mitton 2003).

The second cluster of works that we identified concerns the impact of macroeconomic conditions on the behavior of capital structure determinants at the firm and institutional levels (Zeitun, Temimi, and Mimouni 2017; Alves and Francisco 2015). In particular, the works in this cluster are mainly empirical and use the 2008 global financial crisis to investigate the behavior of the most important capital structure determinants at the firm and institutional levels in the precrisis and postcrisis periods. From a theoretical perspective, pecking order theory and the tradeoff theory are the two reference theories used to formulate the research hypotheses.

In this context, many studies focus on small and medium-sized enterprises (SMEs), analyzing the determinants of SMEs' capital structure in the pre- and postcrisis periods (Van Hoang et al. 2018; Zeitun, Temimi, and Mimouni 2017). The reference work in this cluster is that by Michaelas, Chittenden, and Poutziouris (1999). Specifically, these authors highlight that short-term debt ratios increase during recessions and decrease in economic expansions. Regarding long-term debt ratios, they vary positively with economic growth. Daskalakis, Balios, and Dalla (2017) show that during good economic conditions, short-term debt is impacted more by firm-level variables than by macroeconomic conditions. In contrast, during an economic downturn, macroeconomic variables are more important than firm characteristics. Regarding long-term debt, macroeconomic variables are more important than those at the firm level in any state of the economy, and they become even more important during a crisis.

A Research Agenda for Studying the Capital Structure in Different Macroeconomic States

Based on the SLR and bibliometric analysis that we conducted, the relationship between firm capital structure and macroeconomic conditions has received increasing attention, especially in recent years, following the 2007-2008 global financial crisis and the sovereign debt crisis. The financial crisis offered a natural experiment for investigating the effect of macroeconomic shocks on firm financing decisions. Consequently, we believe that this research field is still relatively young and that further research can be conducted, given that the recent pandemic crisis offers a great opportunity not only to investigate the impacts of this shock on firm capital structure but also to address relevant econometric issues. Unlike the 2007-2008 financial crisis, the pandemic crisis can certainly be considered an exogenous shock, which can make it easier to deal with some typical problems of financial research, i.e., the endogeneity of the variables used in econometric models.

Given the current literature, we believe that the research field we analyzed can be further developed by the following lines of research:

1. Exploring differences at the industry and cross-industry levels. Studies analyzing the impacts of macroeconomic conditions on the capital structure of firms in specific sectors are still limited. Yeh and Roca (2012) investigated the impact of the Asian financial crisis on a sample of Taiwanese petrochemical, textile, and electronics industries. However, capital structure decisions vary from sector to sector and from manufacturing to services, and similarly, changes in macroeconomic conditions affect economic sectors differently. Therefore, the deterioration of and/or improvement in macroeconomic conditions may have a different impact on the capital structure of companies operating in different sectors. Thus, we believe that a better understanding of how macroeconomic conditions influence financial decisions in various sectors is certainly useful not only for scholars to better understand the variety of forms that this phenomenon takes but also for companies to make decisions that better adhere to the specific conditions of the context in which they operate.
2. Analyzing differences at the country and cross-country levels. Although economic globalization has increased the rapid propagation of the expansive or recessive phases of the economy with basically homogeneous effects at the cross-

country level, institutional, social and cultural factors at the country level can undoubtedly affect the intensity of these phases in specific country contexts. Consequently, compared to the current literature, which is mainly focused on some geographical areas (Fattouh, Scaramozzino, and Harris 2005; Dang 2013; Michaelas, Chittenden, and Poutziouris 1999; Yeh and Roca 2012; Korajczyk and Levy 2003), it seems necessary to expand the analysis of this phenomenon to other contexts and to take a cross-country perspective to investigate how and to what extent the characteristics of individual countries impact the relationship between macroeconomic variables and the financial choices of companies (Öztekin and Flannery 2012).

3. Exploring potential mediating and moderating variables. Almost all the papers in our field of interest analyze a simple relationship between macroeconomic conditions and capital structure decisions. However, this methodological choice does not provide a full picture of the mechanisms through which macroeconomic conditions affect financial decisions. Consequently, it would be useful to identify the variables that affect the strength and direction of that relationship (moderators) and the variables that could represent potential channels (mediators) through which macroeconomic events can produce changes in capital structure decisions (Baron and Kenny 1986).
4. Exploring different theoretical approaches. In general, most of the capital structure literature tests predictions derived from pecking order theory and tradeoff theory, which are considered the main competing theoretical approaches to explaining firms' capital structure decisions. However, a growing stream of research in the management literature integrates behavioral aspects to explain firms' decision making. For example, socioemotional wealth is a well-established theoretical approach to explaining the peculiarities of family firms (Gómez-Mejía et al. 2007; Berrone, Cruz, and Gomez-Mejia 2012). Therefore, it would be interesting to combine traditional theoretical approaches that explain capital structure decisions with theories that can better take into account the characteristics of some firm

categories such as family firms, which are a widespread firm category worldwide (Gottardo and Maria Moisello 2014).

5. Investigating in more detail whether and to what extent different types of macroeconomic events differently impact the capital structure and its determinants. Macroeconomic conditions vary as a result of endogenous and exogenous events. Do companies behave the same way in these two situations? Are the determinants of the capital structure the same? Recent studies have investigated the effects of the recent pandemic crisis on firms' financial decisions and have shown that capital structure determinants could behave differently than expected, especially for companies operating in sectors that have been more negatively affected by COVID-19 (i.e., the retail, restaurant, hotel, and transportation industries) (Halling, Yu, and Zechner 2020).

Conclusion

Despite the large capital structure literature, research on the impact of macroeconomic conditions on firm capital structure can be further developed. The 2007-2008 global financial crisis increased interest in the field, and the recent pandemic crisis will most likely prompt scholars to investigate the impacts of this event on the financial structure of firms. Therefore, we believe that a comprehensive review of the literature on the capital structure and macroeconomic conditions is needed to outline the state of the art on the subject to contribute to guiding future research efforts.

In this chapter, we present the results of an SLR on the impact of macroeconomic conditions on firm capital structure decisions by considering the time evolution of the literature and the most cited/recognized papers and authors. In addition to the most influential journals in the field, we show the top contributing institutions/universities and countries where authors are based. Furthermore, the bibliographic mapping created based on cocitation analysis conducted using the HistCite™ software package allow us to identify the main themes or lines of inquiry in the field. Consequently, we present the gaps in the current literature on macroeconomic states and the capital structure as well as a research agenda for future studies on the subject. Therefore, we think that this study contributes to advancing research on the topic by signaling to other scholars the relevant bibliography on the topic and the journals that could serve as potential outlets for their work.

Despite the strengths of this study, we recognize that it suffers from using only the WoS database. Given the recent focus on the topic, we think that this database represents a good starting point for a systematic review of the most relevant literature on the topic. Inevitably, however, it may not have collected all the works published on the topic. Therefore, using other databases could help strengthen the analysis.

REFERENCES

Akhtar, Shumi. (2012). "Capital Structure and Business Cycles." *Accounting & Finance*, *52*, (SUPPL.1), 25–48. https://doi.org/10.1111/j.1467-629X.2011.00425.x.

Alves, Paulo. & Paulo Francisco. (2015). "The Impact of Institutional Environment on the Capital Structure of Firms during Recent Financial Crises." *Quarterly Review of Economics and Finance*, *57* (August), 129–46. https://doi.org/10.1016/j.qref.2014.12.001.

Antoniou, Antonios, Yilmaz Guney. & Krishna Paudyal. (2008). "The Determinants of Capital Structure: Capital Market-Oriented versus Bank-Oriented Institutions." *The Journal of Financial and Quantitative Analysis*, *43* (1), 59–92. https://doi.org/10.2307/27647340.

Baron, Reuben M. & David A Kenny. (1986). "The Moderator-Mediator Variable Distinction in Social Psychological Research: Conceptual, Strategic, and Statistical Considerations." *Journal of Personality and Social Psychology*, *51* (6), 1173–82. https://doi.org/10.1093/alcalc/34.2.197.

Baum, Christopher F., Mustafa Caglayan. & Abdul Rashid. (2017). "Capital Structure Adjustments: Do Macroeconomic and Business Risks Matter?" *Empirical Economics*, *53* (4), 1463–1502. https://doi.org/10.1007/s00181-016-1178-1.

Beck, Thorsten, Asli Demirgüç-Kunt. & Vojislav Maksimovic. (2008). "Financing Patterns around the World: Are Small Firms Different?"

Journal of Financial Economics, *89* (3), 467–87. https://doi.org/10.1016/j.jfineco.2007.10.005.

Berrone, Pascual, Cristina Cruz. & Luis R. Gomez-Mejia. (2012). "Socioemotional Wealth in Family Firms." *Family Business Review*, *25* (3), 258–79. https://doi.org/10.1177/0894486511435355.

Bhamra, Harjoat S., Lars-Alexander Kuehn. & Ilya A. Strebulaev. (2010a). "The Levered Equity Risk Premium and Credit Spreads: A Unified Framework." *Review of Financial Studies*, *23* (2), 645–703. https://doi.org/10.1093/rfs/hhp082.

———. (2010b). "The Aggregate Dynamics of Capital Structure and Macroeconomic Risk." *Review of Financial Studies*, *23* (12), 4187–4241. https://doi.org/10.1093/rfs/hhq075.

Börner, Katy, Chaomei Chen. & Kevin W. Boyack. (2005). "Visualizing Knowledge Domains." *Annual Review of Information Science and Technology*, *37* (1), 179–255. https://doi.org/10.1002/aris.1440370106.

Chen, Hui. (2010). "Macroeconomic Conditions and the Puzzles of Credit Spreads and Capital Structure." *The Journal of Finance*, *65* (6), 2171–2212. https://doi.org/10.1111/j.1540-6261.2010.01613.x.

Choe, Hyuk, Ronald W. Masulis. & Vikram Nanda. (1993). "Common Stock Offerings across the Business Cycle. Theory and Evidence." *Journal of Empirical Finance*, *1* (1), 3–31. https://doi.org/10.1016/0927-5398(93)90003-A.

Cook, Douglas O. & Tian Tang. (2010). "Macroeconomic Conditions and Capital Structure Adjustment Speed." *Journal of Corporate Finance*, *16* (1), 73–87. https://doi.org/10.1016/ j.jcorpfin.2009.02.003.

Dang, Viet Anh. (2013). "An Empirical Analysis of Zero-Leverage Firms: New Evidence from the UK." *International Review of Financial Analysis*, *30*, (December), 189–202. https://doi.org/10.1016/j.irfa.2013.08.007.

Dang, Viet Anh, Minjoo Kim. & Yongcheol Shin. (2014). "Asymmetric Adjustment toward Optimal Capital Structure: Evidence from a Crisis." *International Review of Financial Analysis*, *33*, (May), 226–42. https://doi.org/10.1016/j.irfa.2014.02.013.

Daskalakis, Nikolaos, Dimitrios Balios. & Violetta Dalla. (2017). "The Behaviour of SMEs' Capital Structure Determinants in Different

Macroeconomic States." *Journal of Corporate Finance*, *46*, 248–60. https://doi.org/10.1016/j.jcorpfin.2017.07.005.

Devos, Erik, Upinder Dhillon, Murali Jagannathan. & Srinivasan Krishnamurthy. (2012). "Why Are Firms Unlevered?" *Journal of Corporate Finance*, *18* (3), 664–82. https://doi.org/10.1016/j.jcorpfin.2012.03.003.

Dissanaike, Gishan, Jonathan Faasse. & Ranadeva Jayasekera. (2014). "What Do Equity Issuances Signal? A Study of Equity Issuances in the UK before and during the Financial Crisis." *Journal of International Money and Finance*, *49* (PB), 358–85. https://doi.org/10.1016/j.jimonfin.2014.05.010.

Dittmar, Amy K. & Robert F. Dittmar. (2008). "The Timing of Financing Decisions: An Examination of the Correlation in Financing Waves." *Journal of Financial Economics*, *90* (1), 59–83. https://doi.org/10.1016/j.jfineco.2007.11.007.

Drobetz, Wolfgang, Dirk C. Schilling. & Henning Schröder. (2015). "Heterogeneity in the Speed of Capital Structure Adjustment across Countries and over the Business Cycle." *European Financial Management*, *21* (5), 936–73. https://doi.org/10.1111/eufm.12048.

Ebrahim, M. Shahid, Sourafel Girma, M. Eskandar Shah. & Jonathan Williams. (2014). "Dynamic Capital Structure and Political Patronage: The Case of Malaysia." *International Review of Financial Analysis*, *31*, (January), 117–28. https://doi.org/10.1016/j.irfa.2013.11.004.

Ebrahim, M. Shahid. & Ike Mathur. (2013). "On the Efficiency of the UPREIT Organizational Form: Implications for the Subprime Crisis and CDO's." *Journal of Economic Behavior and Organization*, *85* (1), 286–305. https://doi.org/10.1016/j.jebo.2012.02.015.

Ellul, Andrew, Isil Erel. & Uday Rajan. (2020). "The COVID-19 Pandemic Crisis and Corporate Finance." *The Review of Corporate Finance Studies*, *9* (3), 421–29. https://doi.org/10.1093/ rcfs/cfaa016.

Erel, Isil, Brandon Julio, Woojin Kim. & Michael S. Weisbach. (2012). "Macroeconomic Conditions and Capital Raising." *Review of Financial Studies*, *25* (2), 341–76. https://doi.org/10.1093/rfs/hhr085.

Fattouh, Bassam, Pasquale Scaramozzino. & Laurence Harris. (2005). "Capital Structure in South Korea: A Quantile Regression Approach."

Journal of Development Economics, *76* (1), 231–50. https://doi.org/10.1016/j.jdeveco.2003.12.014.

Ferreira, Fernando A. F. (2018). "Mapping the Field of Arts-Based Management: Bibliographic Coupling and Co-Citation Analyses." *Journal of Business Research*, *85* (April), 348–57. https://doi.org/10.1016/j.jbusres.2017.03.026.

Frank, Murray Z. & Vidhan K Goyal. (2009). "Capital Factors Structure Decisions : Which Are Reliably Important ?" *Financial Management*, *38* (1), 1–37. https://doi.org/10.2139/ssrn.567650.

Gómez-Mejía, Luis R., Katalin Takács Haynes, Manuel Núñez-Nickel, Kathyrn J. L. Jacobson. & José Moyano-Fuentes. (2007). "Socioemotional Wealth and Business Risks in Family-Controlled Firms: Evidence from Spanish Olive Oil Mills." *Administrative Science Quarterly*, *52* (1), 106–37. https://doi.org/10.2189/asqu.52.1.106.

Gottardo, Pietro. & Anna Maria Moisello. (2014). "The Capital Structure Choices of Family Firms: Evidence from Italian Medium-Large Unlisted Firms." *Managerial Finance*, *40* (3), 254–75. https://doi.org/10.1108/MF-03-2013-0065.

Hackbarth, Dirk, Jianjun Miao. & Erwan Morellec. (2006). "Capital Structure, Credit Risk, and Macroeconomic Conditions." *Journal of Financial Economics*, *82* (3), 519–50. https://doi.org/10.1016/j.jfineco.2005.10.003.

Halling, Michael, Jin Yu. & Josef Zechner. (2020). "How Did COVID-19 Affect Firms' Access to Public Capital Markets?" *The Review of Corporate Finance Studies*, *9* (3), 501–33. https://doi.org/10.1093/rcfs/cfaa008.

Hirshleifer, J. (1958). "On the Theory of Optimal Investment Decision." *Journal of Political Economy*, *66* (4), 329–52. https://doi.org/10.1086/258057.

Hoang, Thi Hong Van, Călin Gurău, Amine Lahiani. & Thuy Luu Seran. (2018). "Do Crises Impact Capital Structure? A Study of French Micro-Enterprises." *Small Business Economics*, *50* (1), 181–99. https://doi.org/10.1007/s11187-017-9899-x.

Jensen, Michael C. & William H. Meckling. (1976). "Theory of the Firm: Managerial Behavior, Agency Costs and Ownership Structure." *Journal of Financial Economics*, *3*, 305–60.

Johnson, Simon. & Todd Mitton. (2003). "Cronyism and Capital Controls: Evidence from Malaysia." *Journal of Financial Economics* 67 (2): 351–82. https://doi.org/10.1016/S0304-405X(02)00255-6.

Jong, Abe de, Rezaul Kabir. & Thuy Thu Nguyen. (2008). "Capital Structure around the World: The Roles of Firm- and Country-Specific Determinants." *Journal of Banking and Finance*, *32* (9), 1954–69. https://doi.org/10.1016/j.jbankfin.2007.12.034.

Korajczyk, Robert A. & Amnon Levy. (2003). "Capital Structure Choice: Macroeconomic Conditions and Financial Constraints." *Journal of Financial Economics*, *68* (1), 75–109. https://doi.org/10.1016/S0304-405X(02)00249-0.

Kraus, Sascha, Matthias Breier. & Sonia Dasí-Rodríguez. (2020). "The Art of Crafting a Systematic Literature Review in Entrepreneurship Research." *International Entrepreneurship and Management Journal*, *16* (3), 1023–42. https://doi.org/10.1007/s11365-020-00635-4.

Levy, Amnon. & Christopher Hennessy. (2007). "Why Does Capital Structure Choice Vary with Macroeconomic Conditions?" *Journal of Monetary Economics*, *54* (6), 1545–64. https://doi.org/10.1016/j.jmoneco.2006.04.005.

Linnenluecke, Martina K. (2017). "Resilience in Business and Management Research: A Review of Influential Publications and a Research Agenda." *International Journal of Management Reviews*, *19* (1), 4–30. https://doi.org/10.1111/ijmr.12076.

Lintner, John. (1956). "Distribution of Incomes of Corporations Among Dividends, Retained Earnings, and Taxes." *American Economic Review*, *46* (2), 97–113.

Michaelas, N., Francis Chittenden. & Panikkos Poutziouris. (1999). "Financial Policy and Capital Structure Choice in UK SMEs: Evidence from Company Panel Data." *Small Business Economics 12* (2), 113–130. https://doi.org/http://www.springerlink.com/ content/3durudupbudm/?p=b1297d21ad5d42c084551a122a24031a&pi=75.

Modigliani, Franco. & Merton H. Miller. (1958). "The Cost of Capital, Corporation Finance and the Theory of Investment." *American Economic Review*, *48* (3), 261–97. https://doi.org/10.4013/base.20082.07.

Mokhova, Natalia. & Marek Zinecker. (2014). "Macroeconomic Factors and Corporate Capital Structure." *Procedia - Social and Behavioral Sciences*, *110*, (January), 530–40. https://doi.org/10.1016/j.sbspro.2013.12.897.

Moradi, Amir. & Elisabeth Paulet. (2019). "The Firm-Specific Determinants of Capital Structure – An Empirical Analysis of Firms before and during the Euro Crisis." *Research in International Business and Finance*, *47*, (January), 150–61. https://doi.org/10.1016/j.ribaf.2018.07.007.

Myers, Stewart C. (1977). "Determinants of Corporate Borrowing." *Journal of Financial Economics*, *5* (2), 147–75. https://doi.org/10.1016/0304-405X(77)90015-0.

———. (1984). "The Capital Structure Puzzle." *The Journal of Finance*, *39* (3), 574–92. https://doi.org/10.1111/j.1540-6261.1984.tb03646.x.

Myers, Stewart C. & Nicholas S. Majluf. (1984). "Corporate Financing and Investment Decisions When Firms Have Information That Investors Do Not Have." *Journal of Financial Economics*, *13* (2), 187–221. https://doi.org/10.1016/0304-405X(84)90023-0.

Öhman, Peter. & Darush Yazdanfar. (2017). "Short- and Long-Term Debt Determinants in Swedish SMEs." *Review of Accounting and Finance*, *16* (1), 106–24. https://doi.org/10.1108/RAF-08-2015-0118.

Öztekin, Özde. & Mark J. Flannery. (2012). "Institutional Determinants of Capital Structure Adjustment Speeds." *Journal of Financial Economics*, *103* (1), 88–112. https://doi.org/10.1016/ j.jfineco.2011.08.014.

Proença, Pedro, Raul M. S. Laureano. & Luis M. S. Laureano. (2014). "Determinants of Capital Structure and the 2008 Financial Crisis: Evidence from Portuguese SMEs." *Procedia - Social and Behavioral Sciences*, 182–91. https://doi.org/10.1016/ j.sbspro.2014.09.027.

Rajan, Raghuram G. & Luigi Zingales. (1995). "What Do We Know about Capital Structure? Some Evidence from International Data." *Journal of Finance*, *50* (5), 1421–60. https://doi.org/10.2307/2329322.

Small, Henry. (1973). "Co-citation in the Scientific Literature: A New Measure of the Relationship between Two Documents." *Journal of the American Society for Information Science*, *24* (4), 265–69. https://doi.org/10.1002/asi.4630240406.

Svensson, Göran. (2010). "SSCI and Its Impact Factors: A 'Prisoner's Dilemma'?" *European Journal of Marketing*, *44* (1–2), 23–33. https://doi.org/10.1108/03090561011008583.

Titman, Sheridan. & Roberto Wessels. (1988). "The Determinants of Capital Structure Choice." *Journal of Finance*, *43* (1), 1–19. https://doi.org/10.1111/j.1540-6261.1988.tb02585.x.

Tranfield, David, David Denyer. & Palminder Smart. (2003). "Towards a Methodology for Developing Evidence-Informed Management Knowledge by Means of Systematic Review." *British Journal of Management*, *14* (3), 207–22. https://doi.org/10.1111/1467-8551.00375.

Voutsinas, Konstantinos. & Richard A. Werner. (2011). "Credit Supply and Corporate Capital Structure: Evidence from Japan." *International Review of Financial Analysis*, *20* (5), 320–34. https://doi.org/10.1016/j.irfa.2011.05.002.

Yeh, Hsien Hung. & Eduardo Roca. (2012). "Macroeconomic Conditions and Capital Structure over the Business Cycle: Further Evidence in the Context of Taiwan." In *Emerging Markets Finance and Trade*, *48*, 141–56. M.E. Sharpe Inc. https://doi.org/10.2753/REE1540-496X4805S309.

Zeitun, Rami, Akram Temimi. & Karim Mimouni. (2017). "Do Financial Crises Alter the Dynamics of Corporate Capital Structure? Evidence from GCC Countries." *Quarterly Review of Economics and Finance*, *63*, 21–33. https://doi.org/10.1016/j.qref.2016.05.004

BIOGRAPHICAL SKETCH

Antonio D'Amato

Affiliation: Department of Economics & Statistics – University of Salerno (Italy)

Education: PhD in Public Administration, 2005 – University of Salerno. Dissertation: Financial valuation of public utility firms.

Research and Professional Experience: Antonio has teaching experience at undergraduate and postgraduate levels. He has delivered seminars and talks for industry events and policymakers. As a member of the Department of Economics and Statistics, he is involved in the consulting works of the department.

Professional Appointments: Assistant Professor of Corporate Finance: University of Salerno, Department of Economics & Statistics, December 2016 to Present.

Publications from the Last 3 Years:

Cotugno, M., D'Amato, A., Gallo, A. & Stefanelli, V. (2021). "Do supervisory enforcement actions affect board composition?" *Corporate Governance: An International Review*, *29*(1), 22-44.

D'Amato, A. & Falivena, C. (2020). "Corporate social responsibility and firm value: Do firm size and age matter? Empirical evidence from European listed companies." *Corporate Social Responsibility and Environmental Management*, *27*(2), 909-924.

D'Amato, A. & Gallo, A. (2019). "Bank institutional setting and risk-taking: the missing role of directors' education and turnover." *Corporate Governance: The International Journal of Business in Society*, *19*(4), 774-805.

D'Amato, A. (2020). "Capital structure, debt maturity and financial crisis: Empirical evidence from SMEs." *Small Business Economics*, *55*, 919-941.

Testa, M. & D'Amato, A. (2020). "Does charity affect economic bargaining? Exploring gender × social distance interactions." *Social Responsibility Journal*, *16*(1), 109-128.

In: Advances in Capital Structure Research ISBN: 978-1-53619-948-2
Editor: Karel Marleau

Chapter 3

How do Manufacturing SMEs Rebalance the Short-Term Debt Ratio?

Filipe Sardo[1,2,3] and Zélia Serrasqueiro[4,5]

[1]Department of Economics and Management,
Portucalense University, Rua Dr. António Bernardino de Almeida,
Porto, Portugal
[2]University of Aveiro (ISCA-UA), Portugal
[3]REMIT (Research on Economics, Management
and Information Technologies), Porto, Portugal
[4]Department of Management and Economics,
University of Beira Interior, Estrada do Sineiro,
Covilhã, Portugal
[5] CEFAGE-UBI – Center for Advanced Studies in Management
and Economics of the UBI, Portugal

Abstract

This chapter seeks to analyse SME financing behaviour regarding the adjustment toward the target short-term debt ratio. To reach the paper's objective, using dynamic panel data models, we consider a sample of 8787 SMEs of the manufacturing sector for the period between 2010 and 2017. The results suggest that these firms, after the exhaustion of funds generated internally, rely on short-term debt. The deviation costs seem to imply a fast speed of adjustment to rebalance the short-term debt ratio, avoiding short-term financing imbalance in order to renegotiate credit on favourable terms. The results show that distance from the target short-term debt ratio impacts negatively on the speed of adjustment toward that target ratio. This negative relationship suggests that SMEs distant from the target short-term debt ratio bear transaction costs higher than deviation costs, presenting financing imbalance in the short-run.

Keywords: deviation costs, manufacturing SMEs, target short-term debt ratio, transaction costs

INTRODUCTION

Unlisted small and medium-sized firms (SMEs) face asymmetric information problems due to the lack of financial information disclosure and the firm owner-managed nature. The problems of asymmetric information increase the agency costs of debt, and lenders require collaterals to provide SMEs with long-term loans on favorable terms (Chittenden et al., 1996). However, the firm asset structure determines the capacity to offer collaterals to creditors, consequently the firms' possibility in obtaining long-term loans. Agency costs of debt are generally higher in small firms due to the low level of assets in place, and the difficulty, and costly, of monitoring these firms' activities (Berger and Udell, 1998; Pettit and Singer, 1985).

In this context, various studies (Cressy and Olofsson, 1997, Berger and Udell, 1998; Abor, 2007; Degryse et al., 2012) conclude that SMEs with a higher level of tangible assets experience better terms in obtaining credit. In general, SMEs belonging to the manufacturing sector have an asset structure based on tangible assets (Rao et al., 2019; Serrasqueiro et al., 2011). Accordingly, these firms present a higher capacity to grant collaterals for obtaining long-term loans. However, various studies (Rao et al., 2019; Warmana et al., 2020) conclude that SMEs, namely those belonging to the manufacturing sector, face significant asymmetric information problems that generate problems of adverse selection. When SMEs do not share information regarding their projects with lenders, the latter will offer short-term loans to closely monitor the firm. Moreover, creditors impose severe restrictions on long-term lending loans and making easier the access to short-term loans to SMEs (Lopez-Gracia and Mestre-Barberá, 2015). Consequently, SMEs facing obstacles in accessing long-term debt, and lacking internal finance, may become dependent on short-term debt (Berger and Udell, 1995; Chittenden et al., 1996; Heyman et al., 2008; Bhaird and Lucey, 2014; Lopez-Gracia and Mestre-Barberá, 2015).

SMEs are often managed by their owners seeking to avoid the interference of financiers on firm management (Bhaird and Lucey, 2014). Therefore, it is expected that SMEs rely on short-term debt (Scherr and Hulburt, 2001) to fund their operations. Furthermore, Bhaird and Lucey (2014) conclude that short-term debt allows owners-managers to fund firm needs without losing the firm's autonomy and independence. For those authors, relying on short-term debt, rather than on long-term debt, increases the firm flexibility and autonomy, restricting the firm submission to covenants and avoiding creditors' monitoring (Bhaird and Lucey, 2014; Lopez-Gracia and Mestre-Barberá, 2015). To maintain the control of the firm, SME owners use their personal funds to solve firm liquidity problems. Berger and Udell (1998) concluded that owners' loans are a relevant source of SMEs' financing to overcome liquidity shortfalls.

SMEs can renegotiate short-term credit on favorable terms if they send positive information about the firm financial structure to creditors (Lopez-Gracia and Mestre-Barberá, 2015). Nevertheless, if the information conveyed is negative, creditors will not renegotiate the debt, and they may even demand the firm's liquidation (Scherr and Hulburt, 2001). Accordingly, the predictions of the dynamic trade-off theory (TOT) are important, given that they induce firms to adjust toward target short-term debt ratio, in order to present balanced short-term debt ratios (Taggart, 1977; Jalilvand and Harris, 1984; De Miguel and Pindado, 2001; Ozkan, 2001; Hovakimian et al., 2004; Flannery and Rangan, 2006; Aybar-Arias et al., 2012; Elsas and Florysiak, 2015).

In spite of the importance of short-term debt that, in the current study, refers to bank debt, credit from the suppliers and other creditors obtained by SMEs to fund their operations, the speed of adjustment (SoA) toward the target short-term debt ratio has deserved little attention in the literature on capital structure decisions. This study seeks to fulfil this gap analyzing the SoA and the distance from the target short-term debt ratio in the context of manufacturing SMEs.

SMEs are the cornerstone of the non-financial business economy in Portugal. In 2017, 99,7% of total firms were SMEs, which accounted for 58% turnover and 71,2% of total employment (Central Bank of Portugal, 2018). The manufacturing sector is an important sector of the Portuguese economy, and represented 10% of non-financial businesses, accounting for 25% of total turnover and 24% of employment in 2017 (Central Bank of Portugal, 2018). Considering the importance of manufacturing SMEs for the Portuguese economy, we use a sample of 8787 Portuguese SMEs from this sector of activity between 2010 and 2017.

The results obtained show that manufacturing SMEs adjust quickly toward the target short-term debt ratio. These firms rebalance the short-term debt ratio, sending positive information about the firm, in order to renegotiate credit with favourable terms. However, manufacturing SMEs distant from the target debt ratio seem to bear high transaction costs that negatively affect the speed of adjustment of these firms in rebalancing their short-term debt ratios.

This study has two main contributions to SME capital structure decisions literature. First, considering that SMEs in general, and manufacturing SMEs in particular, are strongly dependent on short-term debt to fund their operations, this study focuses on the speed of adjustment toward the target short-term debt ratio, in order to verify if these firms assure the possibility to renegotiate the credit on favourable terms. Second, the current study analyses the effect of firm owners' loans on the short-term debt ratio. The results show that, despite the importance of retained earnings and short-term debt, owners' loans are also important for manufacturing SMEs to fund operations and probably to solve liquidity shortfalls. Moreover, owners 'loans may be a positive signal about future firm prospects sent to financiers.

The remainder of this chapter is structured as follows. In Section 2, the theoretical framework and research hypotheses are presented. Section 3 presents the methodology used. The results are presented in

Section 4. Section 5 discusses the results, and finally, Section 6 presents the final considerations and implications.

Theoretical Framework and Research Hypotheses

SME financing behaviour seems to follow the predictions of the pecking order theory (POT) (Lopez-Gracia and Aybar-Arias, 2000; Psillaki and Daslakakis, 2009; La Rocca et al., 2011; Mateev and Ivanov, 2013, Rao et al., 2019), i.e., firms prefer retained earnings to fund their needs associated with operations and investments. Consequently, the variations in debt ratios are motivated by firms' need to obtain external finance (Psillaki and Daslakakis, 2009).

The majority of SMEs are managed by their owners that do not target an optimal capital structure (López-Gracia and Aybar-Arias, 2000). The owners-managers of small firms make capital structure decisions intending to avoid third parties' interference in the firm's management (López-Gracia and Aybar-Arias, 2000). Accordingly, SMEs prefer internal finance, followed by debt, and lastly, they issue equity that dilutes the firm's control. The majority of SMEs are outside of the stock market (Ang, 1992; Hutchinson, 1999), and so equity issues are almost unavailable. Therefore, a modified version of POT seems to be followed by SMEs, because financing sources available for these firms are the retained earnings and debt, but equity issues do not almost occur in the context of these firms (Holmes and Kent, 1991). Moreover, SMEs often face constraints in accessing external finance sources, forcing these firms to rely on owners' loans to fund firm needs associated with operations and investments (Berger and Udell, 1998).

The problems of asymmetric information are greater for unlisted SMEs, because of the lack of financial information disclosure and the firm owner-managed nature. Therefore, lenders will require collaterals to provide SMEs with long-term loans on favourable terms (Chittenden et al., 1996). Due to the restrictions in accessing long-term loans, SMEs rely on short-term debt (Heyman et al., 2008; Lopez-Gracia and Mestre-Barberá, 2015). Moreover, Bhaird and Lucey (2014) conclude for a sample of SMEs of thirteen countries that these firms avoid long-term debt in order to preserve their autonomy and independence. Consequently, the level of short-term debt is frequently higher than the level of long-term debt for SMEs.

González and González (2012) conclude that, aside from the financing behaviour according to POT predictions, SMEs also follow TOT in their capital structure decisions. TOT predicts an optimal capital structure that maximizes the debt tax-shields and minimizes the bankruptcy costs generated by debt (Shyam-Sunder and Myers, 1999; Fama and French, 2002; Frank and Goyal, 2008). Debt allows firms to benefit from debt tax-shields (Modigliani and Miller, 1963; DeAngelo and Masulis, 1980) but there are disadvantages associated with debt, namely agency costs, which arise mainly from the potential conflicts between managers/owners and creditors (Jensen and Meckling, 1976; Myers, 1977).

Pettit and Singer (1985) advocate that agency costs of debt are generally higher in small firms with low levels of assets in place, and the monitoring of these firms' activities could be more difficult and expensive. Therefore, small-sized firms, with an asset structure based on tangible assets, may present higher levels of long-term debt, whereas firms with high level of short-term assets may be more dependent on short-term debt (Scherr and Hulburt, 2001). However, SMEs only can renegotiate short-term debt, on favourable terms, if they can send firm positive information to creditors. A way to send positive information about the firm financial condition is based on a balanced capital structure, namely presenting balanced short-term and long-term debt ratios. Accordingly, the predictions of the TOT assume importance, leading firms to target their debt ratios. The target debt ratio is a level of debt according which firms can manage well their risk default, bankruptcy costs and the debt-tax shields. The existence of adjustment/transaction costs may lead firms moving away from their target debt ratios (Taggart, 1977; Jalilvand and Harris, 1984). However, firms would like to adjust toward the target debt ratio, given that a deviation can penalize the firm, like the deterioration of the terms obtained from the creditors.

SMEs bear high transaction costs, justifying a low speed of adjustment of the current short-term debt ratio (López-Gracia and Sogorb-Mira, 2008; González and González, 2012). However, these firms face a high likelihood of bankruptcy, needing to adjust toward target short-term debt ratio to renegotiate credit on favourable terms.

The results of previous studies are not consensual regarding the speed of adjustment toward the target capital structure in the context of SMEs. Heshmati (2001) concludes that deviation costs are inferior to transaction costs for Swedish micro and small and medium-sized firms. Accordingly, these firms adjust slowly and do not perform transactions in the capital market in order to rebalance their capital structures. López-Gracia and Sogorb-Mira (2008) conclude that Spanish small and medium-sized enterprises bear deviation costs lower than the adjustment costs of debt toward target debt level. Therefore, those firms present a low speed of adjustment toward the target debt ratio. However, other studies, like Serrasqueiro et al. (2011) and Sardo and Serrasqueiro (2017), found high speeds of adjustment toward target debt ratios in the context of Portuguese SMEs, suggesting that these firms bear deviation costs superior to adjustment costs. Therefore, it is required the adjustment toward the target short-term debt level to assure the renegotiation of short-term loans. Thus, on the one hand, SMEs may verify a high SoA toward target short-term debt ratio. On the other hand, these firms may face high adjustment costs, which prevent SMEs distant from their target short-term debt ratio to adjust quickly.

Based on the exposed arguments, this study formulates the following research hypotheses:

Hypothesis 1 (H1): SMEs present a high SoA toward target short-term debt ratio.

Hypothesis 2 (H2): SMEs distant from the target short-term debt ratio bear high adjustment costs, which implies a SoA.

METHODOLOGY

Database and Variables

In the present study, we use data for SMEs of the manufacturing sector, for the period between 2010 to 2017, gathered from the SABI database supplied by Bureau van Dijk's. SABI database contains economic and financial information on Iberian firms. In the current study, the firms that compose the research sample meet the European Commission's definition for SMEs (Recommendation 2003/36/CE). According to the recommendation, a business unit is considered an SME when: (i) it employs fewer than 250 people; and (ii) a turnover under €50 million and/or total assets under €43 million.

Table 1. Variables and measurement

Variables	Term	Measurement
Dependent variable:		
Short-term Debt Ratio	$SDebt_{i,t}$	Ratio of short-term debt to total assets
Capital structure determinants		
Owners' loans	$OwnLoans_{i,t}$	Ratio of shareholders' loans to total assets
Profit	$PROF_{i,t}$	Ratio of operating income before depreciation to total assets
Non-Debt Tax Shields	$NDTS_{i,t}$	Ratio of depreciations to fixed assets
Tangibility	$TANG_{i,t}$	Ratio of fixed assets to total assets
Growth Opportunities	$GO_{i,t}$	Ratio of intangible assets to total assets
Size	$SIZE_{i,t}$	Logarithm of total assets
Age	$AGE_{i,t}$	Logarithm of the number of years of firm life
Business Risk	$RISK_{i,t}$	Ratio of standard deviation of operating profits less mean of operating profits to total assets
Distance between target short-term debt ratio [1] and observed short-term debt ratio	$\text{Distance} - \text{speedsd}_{i,t}$	Discrete variable with the value 1(0) if $\lvert \text{SDebt}^*_{i,t} - \text{SDebt}_{i,t} \rvert$ is above (below) the mean of the whole sample

The proxies considered for the determinants of short-term debt have been used in various earlier studies (Michaelas et al., 1999; Sogorb-Mira 2005; Heyman et al., 2008; López-Gracia and Sogorb-Mira, 2008; Degryse et al., 2012). Following, Berger and Udell (1998) and Coleman (2006) we also consider owners' loans as an explanatory variable.

We drop the SMEs with less than five years of continuous observations over the period of analysis. To control for the possible influence of outliers, we drop the observations in the one per cent tails for each of the regression variables.

The research sample is composed of 8787 Portuguese SMEs of the manufacturing sector, presenting an unbalanced structure, and the number of years of observations for each firm varies between five and eight. The use of unbalanced panels allows the entry and exit of firms randomly in the panel, mitigating partially the potential problem of survivor bias.

Regarding the proxies of the research variables, for short-term debt ratio, we selected the proxy frequently used in the empirical literature (Chittenden et al., 1996; Michaelas et al., 1999; Sogorb-Mira, 2005) as presented in Table 1. The determinants of short-term debt are proxied by the research variables presented in Table 1.

Estimation Method

To analyse the SoA of SMEs, we use the following partial adjustment model:

$$SDebt_{i,t} - SDebt_{i,t-1} = \beta_0 + \alpha(SDebt^{*}_{i,t} - SDebt_{i,t-1}) \tag{1}$$

where: $Debt_{i,t}$ is the short-term debt of firm i in the current period; $SDebt_{i,t-1}$ is the short-term debt of firm i in the previous period; $SDebt^{*}_{i,t}$ is the optimal short-term debt of firm i in the current period; and α is the speed of adjustment of the current level of short-term debt ratio toward target level. Therefore, the dynamic character of capital structure decisions is considered in the model presented in equation (1).

As Shyam-Sunder and Myers (1999) state, the optimal level of debt depends on firms' specific characteristics, such as size, profitability and others. Following De Miguel and Pindado (2001), Ozkan (2001), Fama and French (2002) and Gaud et al. (2005), Lopéz-Gracia and Sogorb-Mira (2008), this study considers that optimal debt depends on firms' specific characteristics.

Therefore, the model for firms' optimal level of short-term debt is given by:

$$SDebt_{i,t}^{*} = \sum_{K=1}^{n} \varphi_K Z_{K,i,t} + \mu_t d_t + \mu_i + v_{i,t} \quad (2)$$

Where $Z_{K,i,t}$ is the determinant k of the short-term debt of firm i at time t, φ_K are the coefficients of each determinant of short-term debt, μ_t are the coefficients of each temporal dummy variable, d_t represents time effects regarding possible changes in the economic situation, μ_i are the firms' specific factors, that are not directly observable by the determinants of short-term debt and $v_{i,t}$is the error with zero average and constant variance.

Substituting (2) in (1) respectively, and regrouping the terms, we obtain:

$$SDebt_{i,t} = \lambda SDebt_{i,t-1} + \sum_{K=1}^{n} \beta_k Z_{k,i,t} + \mu_t d_t + \mu_i + v_{i,t} \quad (3)$$

Where: $\lambda = (1 - \alpha)$ and $\beta_k = \alpha \varphi_K$.

It is particularly important to estimate correctly the relationships between short-term debt in the current period and short-term debt in the previous period, in order to estimate the adjustment toward target short-term debt ratio. Estimating the equation (3) on the basis of traditional panel methods, considering fixed or random individual effects, we obtain biased and inconsistent estimates, since besides the correlation between non-observable individual effects (μ_i) and short-term debt in the previous period ($SDebt_{i,t-1}$), there is also a correlation between $v_{i,t}$ and $SDebt_{i,t-1}$, which implies that the firms' non-observable individual effects and the error are correlated with lagged short-term debt. The use of dynamic panel estimators allows us to eliminate these correlations, since (i) use of the variables, in first differences allows the elimination of the correlation between non-observable individual effects (μ_i) and the lagged dependent variable ($SDebt_{i,t-1}$); and (ii) use of instrumental variables (lagged dependent and independent variables) allows the elimination of the correlation between the error $v_{i,t}$ and the lagged dependent variable ($SDebt_{i,t-1}$). Arellano and Bond (1991) suggest that the use of dynamic panel estimators has the following extra advantages: (i) mitigation of endogeneity; (ii) greater control of possible collinearity between independent variables; and (iii) lessening the problem of neglecting explanatory variables.

When the dependent variable is persistent, i.e., when there is a strong correlation between short-term debt in the current period and short-term debt in the previous period, Blundell and Bond (1998) conclude that the system generalized methods of moments dynamic estimator (hereafter, GMM-Sys) is clearly appropriate, mitigating the bias in the estimated results. In this study, the correlation of the coefficient between short-term debt in the current period and short-term debt in the previous period is 0.8681. This value indicates that short-term debt is persistent and, thereby the GMM-Sys is the most appropriate estimator in comparison to the difference generalized methods of moments dynamic estimator (hereafter, GMM-Dif). This being so, use of the GMM-Sys seems to be the most appropriate way to estimate the relationships between short-term debt and its determinants rather than using the GMM -Dif. Therefore, as a method of estimation, we use the GMM-Sys. Moreover, the results of the GMM-Sys will be considered robust, if the restrictions imposed by using the instruments are valid, as well as there is absence of second-order autocorrelation.

RESULTS

Descriptive Statistics and Correlation Matrix

Table 2 presents the descriptive statistics regarding the dependent and explanatory variables for SMEs of the manufacturing sector.

Considering the average of total assets about 1,63 million euros (Table 2), we may conclude that the sample is mainly composed of small-sized firms, and they are on average 19 years old. The average of profitability is about 9,2%, and the short-term debt represents 42,5% of total assets, indicating that SMEs of the manufacturing sector depend on short-term debt. Moreover, the average of owners' loans is around 1,2%, and the average of tangible assets is around 27%. The average growth opportunities is low (0.2%) suggesting a low level of investment opportunities, in the context of manufacturing SMEs. Table 3 presents the correlation matrix of the variables.

Table 2. Descriptive statistics

Variables	Observations	Mean	Std. Dev.	Min	Max
$SDebt_{i,t}$	8787	.42494	.20205	0	.98843
$PROF_{i,t}$	8787	.092389	.08755	-2.7474	.89107
$OwnLoans_{i,t}$	8787	.012165	.05865	0	.79119
$TANG_{i,t}$	8787	.27185	.2015	0	.99578
$GO_{i,t}$	8787	.002364	.01017	0	.24659
$NDTS_{i,t}$	8787	.039339	.03067	0	.43581
$SIZE_{i,t}$	8787	14.3039	1.3082	6.2146	16.64
$AGE_{i,t}$	8787	2.951652	.68452	0	4.248
$Risk_{i,t}$	8787	-.045643	.07258	-.397456	2.0368

Gujarati and Porter (2010) conclude that the problem of collinearity between explanatory variables may be particularly relevant when the correlation coefficients between variables are over 50%. As we can see from Table 3, corresponding to the correlation matrix between the variables used in this study, the correlation coefficients between the independent variables are in no circumstances over 50%, therefore, problems of possible collinearity between independent variables seem not be a significant threat in this study.

Table 3. Correlation matrix

	$SDebt_{i,t}$	$PROF_{i,t}$	$OwnLoans_{i,t}$	$TANG_{i,t}$	$GO_{i,t}$	$NDTS_{i,t}$	$SIZE_{i,t}$	$AGE_{i,t}$	$Risk_{i,t}$
$SDebt_{i,t}$	1.00								
$PROF_{i,t}$	-0.071***	1.00							
$OwnLoans_{i,t}$	0.183***	-0.07***	1.00						
$TANG_{i,t}$	-0.19***	0.032**	0.002	1.00					
$GO_{i,t}$	-0.0275	-0.005	-0.01	0.05***	1.00				
$NDTS_{i,t}$	-0.033**	0.39***	-0.04***	0.39***	0.076***	1.00			
$SIZE_{i,t}$	0.109***	0.18***	-0.21***	-0.009	-0.046**	0.04***	1.00		
$AGE_{i,t}$	-0.242***	-0.13***	-0.03	0.03***	-0.0213	-0.115***	0.24***	1.00	
$Risk_{i,t}$	0.0319	-0.53***	0.11***	-0.1***	0.008	-0.31***	-0.34***	0.03	1.00

1. *** statistical significance at the 1% level. 2. ** statistical significance at the 5% level

Table 4. Adjustment towards target short-term debt ratio (estimations from system GMM 1998)

Independent variables	Dependent variable: $\mathbf{SDebt_{i,t}}$
$SDebt_{i,t-1}$	0.2557*** (0.05746)
$PROF_{i,t}$	-0.2318*** (0.02922)
$OwnLoans_{i,t}$	0.3294*** (0.1171)
$TANG_{i,t}$	-0.08628*** (0.01598)
$GO_{i,t}$	-0.08775 (0.1436)
$NDTS_{i,t}$	0.1593 (0.1926)
$SIZE_{i,t}$	0.02230*** (0.002562)
$AGE_{i,t}$	-0.04596*** (0.005640)
$Risk_{i,t}$	0.1131*** (0.02738)
$Distance - Speedsd_{i,t}$	-0.2005*** (0.02737)
$Distance - Speedsd_{i,t} * SDebt_{i,t-1}$	0.4673*** (0.05597)
CONS	0.1649*** (0.03763)
Observations	8787
Number of firms	1612
Wald Statistics	2486.8***
AR(1) test (p-value)	-5.2540***
AR(2) test (p-value)	0.8240
Hansen test (χ^2)	67.306

Notes: 1. CONS is the constant of the regressions. 2. Standard deviations in () parenthesis. 3. *** statistical significance at the 1% level. 4. The estimates include industry sector *dummy* variables, but not shown. 5. The estimates include time *dummy* variables, but not shown. 6.AR(1) test is a test of first- order autocorrelation in the first-differenced residuals and is distributed as N(0,1), under the null hypothesis of no first-order autocorrelation. 7. AR(2) test is a test of second-order autocorrelation in the first-differenced residuals and is distributed as N(0,1), under the null hypothesis of no second-order autocorrelation.8.

Hansen test (χ^2) of over-identification is under the null hypothesis that all instruments are valid

Speed of Adjustment toward Target Short-Term Debt Ratio and Determinants of Short-Term Debt Ratio

Table 4 presents the results regarding the adjustments of current short-term debt of SMEs of the manufacturing sector. Also, we present the relationships between determinants and the short-term debt ratio.

The results for the Hansen test indicate that we cannot reject the null hypothesis of the validity of instruments. Also, we cannot reject the null hypothesis of the absence of second-order autocorrelation. Considering the validity of the instruments as well as the absence of second-order autocorrelation, we may conclude that the results obtained based on the GMM-Sys are robust and open to discussion.

The results of Table 4 suggest that SMEs of the manufacturing sector adjust current short-term debt ratio toward the respective target ratio. Regarding the relationships between determinants and short-term debt ratio, we find that short-term debt in the previous period, owners' loans, size, non-debt tax shields and risk are positively related to short-term debt in the current period. In contrast, profitability, tangibility, and age are negatively related to short-term debt in the current period.

RESULTS DISCUSSION

Speed of Adjustment toward Target Short-Term Debt Ratio

The results show that the speed of adjustment toward the target short-term debt ratio is $\alpha = 74.43\%$. This result evidences a high level of adjustment of short-term debt ratio for SMEs of the manufacturing sector, therefore we cannot reject the hypothesis 1 formulated before. A speed of adjustment of 74.43% is high, suggesting these firms bear deviation costs higher than transaction costs. Therefore, manufacturing SMEs adjust quickly, to rebalance the short-term debt ratio, probably, to renegotiate credit on favourable terms. Sardo and Serrasqueiro (2017) obtained a similar speed of adjustment toward target short-term debt ratio for Portuguese SMEs of various activity sectors: a speed of adjustment toward the target short-term debt ratio of 71.8% and 67.2% for medium-sized and small firms, respectively. Lemma and Negash (2014) found a speed of adjustment toward short-term debt about 56.3% for manufacturing firms within the context of developing economies. Gonzalez and Gonzalez (2012) obtained a SoA toward target total debt ratio around 60% for Spanish small and medium-sized firms. Dang et al., (2012) identified a SoA toward target total debt ratio about 77% for UK small firms.

Distance, here considered as a determinant of the speed of adjustment, influences negatively the speed of adjustment toward the target short-term debt ratio. This negative relationship suggests that SMEs distant from the target short-term debt ratio bear transaction costs higher than deviation costs. Therefore, we cannot reject the hypothesis 2 previously formulated. SMEs far from the target short-term debt ratio are not motivated to rebalance their short-term debt ratio, staying away from the target ratio.

However, the results of the previous studies about the impact of the distance on the speed of adjustment are heterogeneous. Sardo and Serrasqueiro (2017) obtained a similar result of the current study, when analysing the impact of distance on the SoA toward target short-term debt ratio for Portuguese SMEs. Lööf (2004) and Aybar-Arias et al. (2012) also found a negative effect of distance on the speed of adjustment toward target total debt ratio for large British firms and Spanish SMEs, respectively. Heshmati (2001) found a positive relationship between distance and the SoA toward target total debt for Swedish micro, and small and medium-sized firms. Also, Drobetz and Wanzenried (2006) identify a positive relationship between distance and SoA toward target total debt ratio in German, French, Italian and British firms, while Lemma and Negash (2014) found a positive but not statistically significant relationship between distance and the SoA toward target short-term debt ratio in firms located in developing countries in Africa.

Determinants of Short-Term Debt Ratio

Regarding the relationships between the determinants and short-term debt ratio, the results show a negative relationship between profitability and short-term debt, suggesting that more profitable SMEs are less dependent on short-term debt. The positive relationship between owners' loans and short-term debt, suggest that owners´loans contribute to mitigate the firm liquidity shortfalls. Owners' loans imply low costs and at the same time they are a positive signal about the firm future prospects for creditors. Therefore, manufacturing SMEs seem to follow the predictions of POT in their capital structure decisions. These results corroborate the results of previous studies (López-Gracia and Aybar-Arias, 2000; Öhman and Yazdanfar, 2017; D´Amato, 2020), concluding that SMEs rely on retained earnings to fund the operations and investments at a low cost, preserving the firm independence and autonomy (Hutchinson 1999; Sogorb-Mira, 2005).

The negative impact of tangibility on short-term debt was expected, suggesting that SMEs follow the matching principle, i.e., they match the maturity of their assets with the maturity of the sources that fund those assets. A similar relationship was found in previous studies (Chittenden et al., 1996; Hall et al., 2004; Sogorb-Mira, 2005; Mateev and Ivanov, 2013; D´Amato, 2020). Firm size influences positively the short-term debt level, corroborating the results of previous studies (Mateev and Ivanov, 2013; Degryse et al., 2012; D´Amato, 2020), indicating that larger SMEs use more short-term debt because their greater bargaining power with creditors (Mateev and Ivanov, 2013). Lopez-Gracia and Mestre-Barberá (2015) identified a positive relationship between size and short-term debt level, concluding that lenders prefer to lend short-term loans to smaller firms to closely monitor and more accurately assess the possibility of renewing a loan.

The results here obtained suggest that older SMEs have a high capacity to generate internal funds, reducing the dependence on short-term debt. An identical result was identified by Bhaird and Lucey (2014), concluding that older firms have a greater capacity to generate retained earnings, reducing the dependence on short-term debt. It is worthy to enhance the positive effect of risk on short-term debt, suggesting that riskier SMEs are more dependent on short-term debt. This may be explained by the inexistence of alternative external finance sources, forcing riskier manufacturing SMEs to rely on the short-term debt to fund their needs.

Conclusion

This chapter purpose was to analyse the SME financing behaviour, regarding the adjustments toward the target short-term debt ratio. To reach the paper's objective, using dynamic panel data models, we consider a sample of 8787 SMEs of the manufacturing sector for the period between 2010 and 2017.

The results obtained indicate that SMEs of the manufacturing sector present a high speed of adjustment toward target short-term debt ratio, suggesting the need to avoid short-term financing imbalance. This financing behaviour of manufacturing SMEs is according to the predictions of dynamic trade-off theory. However, these firms also follow the predictions of the pecking order theory, given that profitability impacts negatively on short-term debt. Moreover, the results suggest that after the exhaustion of retained earnings, manufacturing SMEs rely on short-term debt. Owners' loans impact positively on short-term debt, thus manufacturing SME owners-managers seem fund their firms, in order to preserve the firm's control and independence.

The dependence of manufacturing SMEs on short-term debt may require to adjust quick toward target short-term debt ratio, avoiding financing imbalance in order to renegotiate credit with favourable terms. However, SMEs distant from the target short-term debt ratio face high transaction costs that prevents these firms to rebalance quickly their short-term debt ratios.

The current study suggests to policymakers to promote the access to alternative external finance sources by manufacturing SMEs, in order to allow the reduction of transaction costs, as well as a quicker rebalance of SME short-term debt ratios. This study has limitations, namely, the analysis focused only upon only one sector of activity. Moreover, another limitation is related to the use of secondary data that prevents to analyse the relationships between the characteristics of SME owners-managers and capital structure decisions. For future research, we suggest the analysis of SME capital structure decisions, in the context of various industries. Also, for future research, we suggest to analyse the speed adjustment toward target short term debt ratio, differentiating between financially constrained with non-financially constrained SMEs.

REFERENCES

Abor, J. (2007). Debt policy and performance of SMEs: evidence from Ghanaian and South Africa firms. *Journal of Risk Finance*, *8*, 364-79.

Ang, J. (1992). On the theory of finance for privately held firms. *The Journal of Small Business Finance*, *1*(3), 185-203.

Arellano, M. & Bond, S. (1991). Some tests of specification for panel data: Monte Carlo evidence and an application to employment equations. *Review of Economic Studies*, *58*, 277-297.

Aybar-Arias, C., Casino-Martinez, A. & Lopez-Gracia, J. (2012). On the adjustment speed of SMEs to their optimal capital structure. *Small Business Economics*, *39*(4), 977-996.

Berger, A. & Udell, G. (1995). Relationship lending and lines of credit in small firm finance. *Journal of Business*, *68*, 351-382.

Berger, A. N. & Udell, G. F. (1998). The economics of small business finance: the roles of private equity and debt markets in the financial growth cycle. *Journal of Banking and Finance*, *22*, 613-673.

Bhaird, C. & Lucey, B. (2014). Culture's influences: An investigation of inter-country differences in capital structure. *Borsa Istanbul Review*, *14*(1), 2014, 1-9.

Blundell, M. & Bond, S. (1998). Initial conditions and moment restrictions in dynamic panel data models. *Journal of Econometrics*, *87*, 115-143.

Central Bank of Portugal. (2018). Análise setorial das sociedades não financeiras em Portugal | 2017. *Estudos da Central de Balanços*, Banco de Portugal. [Sectoral analysis of non-financial corporations in Portugal | 2017. *Studies by the Central Balance-Sheet Database*, Banco de Portugal.]

Chittenden, H., Hall, G. & Hutchinson, P. (1996). Small firm growth, access to capital markets and financial structure: review of issues and an empirical investigation. *Small Business Economics*, *8*, 59-67.

Coleman, S. (2006). Capital structure in small manufacturing firms: evidence from the data, *Journal of Entrepreneurial Finance and Business Ventures*, *11* (3), 105-122.

Cressy, R. & Olofsson, C. (1997). The financial conditions for Swedish SMEs: survey and research agenda. *Small Business Economics*, *9*, 179-194.

D'Amato, A. (2020). Capital structure, debt maturity, and financial crisis: empirical evidence from SMEs. *Small Business Economics*, *55*, 919–941.

Dang, V., Kim, M. & Shin, Y. (2012). Asymmetric capital structure adjustments: New evidence from dynamic panel threshold models. *Journal Empirical Finance*, *19*, 465-482.

De Miguel, A. & Pindado, J. (2001). Determinants of capital structure: new evidence from Spanish panel data. *Journal of Corporate Finance*, *7* (1), 77-99.

DeAngelo, H. & Masulis, R. (1980). Optimal capital structure under corporate and personal taxation. *Journal of Financial Economics*, *8* (1), 3-29.

Degryse, H., Goeij, P. & Kappert, P. (2012). The impact of firm and industry characteristics on small firm's capital structure. *Small Business Economics*, *38*, 431-447.

Drobetz, W., and Wanzenried, G. (2006). What determines the speed of adjustment to the target capital structure? *Applied Financial Economics*, 16(13), 941–958.

Elsas, R. & Florysiak, D. (2015). Dynamic capital structure adjustment and the impact of fractional dependent variables. *Journal of Financial and Quantitative Analysis*, *50* (05), 1105–1133.

Fama, E. & French, K. (2002). Testing trade-off and pecking-order predictions about dividends and debt. *The Review of Financial Studies*, *Spring*, *15* (1), 1-33.

Flannery, M. & Rangan, K. (2006). Partial adjustment toward target capital structures. *Journal of Financial Economics*, *79*(3), 469–506.

Frank, M., and Goyal, V. (2008). Trade-off and pecking-order theories of debt in E. Eckbo (ed.), *Handbook of Corporate Finance - Empirical Corporate Finance*, 2, 135-197. Elsevier Science.

Gaud, P., Jani, E., Hoesli, M. & Bender, A. (2005). The capital structure of Swiss companies: an empirical analysis using dynamic panel data. *European Financial Management*, *11*(1), 51-69.

González, V. & González, F. (2012). Firm size and capital structure: evidence using dynamic panel data. *Applied Economics*, *44*, 4745–4754.

Gujarati, D. & Porter, D. (2010). *Essentials of Econometrics*. 4th ed. New York: McGraw – Hill International.

Heshmati, A. (2001). On the growth of micro and small firms: evidence from Sweden. *Small Business Economics*, *17*, 213-228.

Heyman, D., Deloof M. & Ooghe, H. (2008). The financial structure of private held Belgian firms. *Small Business Economics*, *30*, 301-313.

Holmes, S. & Kent, P. (1991). An empirical analysis of the financial structure of small and large Australian manufacturing enterprises. *The Journal of Small Business Finance*, *1*, 141-154.

Hutchinson, P. (1999). Small enterprise: finance ownership and control. *International Journal of Management Reviews*, *1* (3), 343-365.

Hovakimian, A., Hovakimian, G. & Tehranian, H. (2004). Determinants of target capital structure: The case of dual debt and equity issues. *Journal of Financial Economics*, *71* (3), 517–540.

Jalilvand, A. & Harris, R. (1984). Corporate behavior in adjusting to capital structure and dividend targets: an econometric study. *The Journal of Finance*, *39*, 127–145.

Jensen, J. & Meckling, W. (1976). Theory of the firm: managerial behavior, agency costs and ownership structure. *Journal of Financial Economics*, *3* (4), 305-360.

La Rocca, M., La Rocca, T. & Cariola, A. (2011). Capital structure decisions during a firm's life cycle. *Small Business Economics*, *37*, 107-130.

Lemma, T. & Negash, M. (2014). Determinants of the adjustment speed of capital structure. *Journal of Applied Accounting Research*, *15*, 64–99.

Lööf, H. (2004). Dynamic optimal capital structure and technical change. *Structural Change and Economic Dynamics*, *15* (4), 449-468.

López-Gracia, J. & Aybar-Arias, C. (2000). An empirical approach to the financial behaviour of small and medium sized companies. *Small Business Economics*, *14*, 55-63.

López-Gracia, J. & Sogorb-Mira, F. (2008). Testing trade-off and pecking-order theories financing SMEs. *Small Business Economics*, *31*, 117-136.

Lopez-Gracia, J. & Mestre-Barberá, R. (2015). On the relevance of agency conflicts in SME debt maturity structure. *Journal of Small Business Management*, *53*, 714-734.

Mateev, M., Poutziouris, P. & Ivanov, K. (2013). On the determinants of SME capital structure of Eastern and Central Europe-a dynamic panel analysis. *Research in International Business and Finance*, *27* (1), 28-51.

Michaelas, N., Chittenden, F. & Poutziouris, P. (1999). Financial policy and capital structure choice in U.K. SMEs: empirical evidence from company panel data. *Small Business Economics*, *12*, 113-130.

Modigliani, F. & Miller, M. (1963). Corporate income taxes and the cost of capital: a correction. *The American Economic Review*, *53* (3), 433-443.

Myers, S. (1977). Determinants of corporate borrowing. *Journal of Financial Economics*, *5*, November, 147-175.

Öhman, P. & Yazdanfar, D. (2017). Short- and long-term debt determinants in Swedish SMEs. *Review of Accounting and Finance*, *16*(1), 106-124.

Ozkan, A. (2001). Determinants of capital structure and adjustment to long run target: evidence from UK company panel data. *Journal of Business Finance & Accounting*, *28* (1), 175-198.

Pettit, R. & Singer, R. (1985). Small business finance: a research agenda. *Financial Management*, *14* (3), 47- 60.

Psillaki, M. & Daskalakis, N. (2009). Are the determinants of capital structure country of firm specific? Evidence from SMEs. *Small Business Economics*, *33* (3), 319-333.

Rao, P., Kumar, S. & Madhavan, V. (2019), A study on factors driving the capital structure decisions of small and medium enterprises (SMEs) in India, *IIMB Management Review*, *31*(1), 37-50.

Sardo, F. & Serrasqueiro, Z. (2017). Does dynamic trade-off theory explain Portuguese SME capital structure decisions? *Journal of Small Business and Enterprise Development*, *24* (3), 485-502.

Scherr, F. & Hulburt, H. (2001). *The debt maturity structure of small firms. Financial Management*, Spring, 85-111.

Serrasqueiro, Z., Armada, M. & Maçãs Nunes, P. (2011). Pecking order theory versus trade-off theory: are service SMEs' capital structure decisions different? *Service Business*, *5*(4), 381-409.

Shyam-Sunder, L. & Myers, S. (1999). Testing static trade-off against pecking-order models of capital structure. *Journal of Financial Economics*, *51*, 219-244.

Sogorb-Mira, F. (2005). How SME uniqueness affects capital structure: evidence from a 1994-1998 Spanish data panel. *Small Business Economics*, *25*, 447-457.

Taggart, R. (1977). A model of corporate financing decisions. *The Journal of Finance*, *32*, 1467–1484.

Warmana, G., Rahyuda, I. & Purbawangsa, I. (2020). Investigating capital structure speed of adjustment (SOA) of Indonesian companies for corporate value. *Global Journal of Flexible Systems Management*, *21*, 215–231.

In: Advances in Capital Structure Research ISBN: 978-1-53619-948-2
Editor: Karel Marleau

Chapter 4

THE INFLUENCE OF REGULATION ON DEBT MATURITY STRUCTURE AND RISK MANAGEMENT FOR EUROPEAN BANKS

Elisabeth Paulet[1,*], PhD, Miia Chabot[2], PhD and Tamym Abdessemed[3], PhD

[1]ICN Business School, Nancy, France
[2]Essca School of Management, Angers, France
[3]ISIT, Paris France

ABSTRACT

Since the beginning of the European banking integration in November 2014, debt structure has become essential in the bank capitalization process. This chapter discusses the way in which debt structure (short- and long-term) affects capitalization, risk management and, consequently, the business model of banks. The apparent disconnection between the market valuation of risky assets held by banks and their book value is investigated through the cross-use of market variables against more standard accounting data.

* Corresponding Author's E-mail: elisabeth.paulet@icn-groupe.fr.

In order to better understand the type of restructuring now under way in the major European Banks, we run a Panel OLS to analyze the capitalization process using a broad panel of 133 banks covering the period 2000-2017, and a smaller sample composed of the largest institutions. Our finding is that both short- and long-term debt has a major effect on bank capitalization. The most vulnerable institutions are those with substantial levels of short-term debt and significant volumes of non-performing assets. Long-term debt, in contrast, allows banks to be more resilient. Regulators should therefore pay particular attention to the way banks handle their volumes of non-performing loans to ensure overall stability.

1. INTRODUCTION

Since the beginning of the European banking integration in November 2014, European banks have lost almost half of their market capitalization (Acharya et al., 2016). There remain a number of risks to be addressed about their balance sheets. Such risks would necessitate a more substantial recapitalization exercise. Yet, as a large part of the literature argues, the stricter prudential requirements in Europe are overly restrictive for banks, with perverse effects for the system. Arriving at the "adequate" capitalization balance therefore lies at the core of the agenda.

The aim of this chapter is to investigate in detail the market capitalization process and debt structure of European banks. This process is examined through two different perspectives. First, we aim to produce an overview of the current situation using a significant panel of banks covering the 2000-2017 period. Second, we take up the most significant banks in this sample for further investigation. Different explanatory lenses are employed. The apparent disconnection between the market valuation of risky assets held by banks and their book value is investigated through the cross-use of market variables against more standard accounting data. Because regulatory changes are now prompting European banking institutions to reorganize their business model, we focus on the structure of their short- and long-term debt. The extent to which institutions organize their liabilities considerably influences their market capitalization (Cetina et al., 2015). Working with a reduced sample of representative financial institutions using data analytics makes it possible to identify clusters of representative practices. Comparisons between the major institutions are therefore proposed, enabling a better understanding of the current stakes in the capitalization process at work in Europe.

Our approach is informed by three distinct strands in the literature. The first relates bank capitalization to the profitability and efficiency of banking institutions (Bitar et al., 2018, Chortareas et al., 2012, Fiordelisi et al., 2011; Altunbas et al., 2007). The second addresses the adverse effects of overly stringent prudential requirements through the notions of credit risk transfer and credit crunch (Thornton and di Tommaso, 2018, Roulet 2018; Beyhaghi et al, 2017, Rodrìguez Gil et al., 2015). The last group concentrates on the measurement of the risk to which the banks are exposed and the impact of this on the bank's business model (Cucinelli et al., 2018; Gonzalèz et al., 2016; Iannotta et al., 2007). The specific contribution of our work is to mobilize a new set of indicators to investigate the market capitalization process of banks, while also covering a significantly longer period of time.

Our results suggest that European banks' market capitalization is greatly impacted by the ability of banks not to default on their market engagements. Investor confidence is essential to the capitalization dynamics of banks. In addition, debt structure (short-term and long-term) is shown to be a decisive factor. Ultimately, we demonstrate that concerns regarding risky assets in banks' balance sheets remain a thorny issue. From our results, non-performing loans do not seem to exhibit a significant influence on capitalization. Thus, there is scope for further refinements in prudential banking regulation to ensure that banks will be less exposed to credit risks in addition to capital requirements.

The rest of this chapter is organized as follows. Section 2 presents an overview of the literature and discusses the main findings to date with respect to European banks and capitalization. Section 3 introduces the data and the empirical methodology chosen. Section 4 details and discusses the panel analysis, and the principal component analysis. Section 5 provides our conclusions and final considerations.

2. Literature Review

The changes in banking prudential regulations in Europe are bringing about shifts in credit practices, the full implications of which have not been fully addressed in the literature. The banks are actually transferring their risks and restructuring their debts, and this considerably influences their market capitalisation process. Table 1 offers a summary of the recent literature on these matters. This chapter reviews market capitalization and balance sheet fundamentals to evaluate the implications in terms of risk management for banking institutions. This innovative approach makes it possible to discuss the influence of the regulatory tools considered in the previous literature. It provides an opportunity to address the way the financial market alters the banking institutions' strategies for transferring credit risk. Since regulatory ratios in Europe are an essential factor behind these new practices, our literature review also examines the mechanisms at work in the balance-sheet structures of the banks. The evidence points to a fundamental reshaping of credit risk transfer strategies. Such strategies alter the structure of short- and long-term debt held by banks. These strategies also affect the liquidity risk to which banks are exposed.

2.1. Basel III and Its Consequences for Banking Credit Practices in Europe

The implementation of the Basel Accords has given rise to a substantial body of literature, essentially directed towards the effects that capital requirements have on banks' behaviour. The relationship linking a bank's capital to the volumes of loans it provides was among the first topics addressed (Roulet, 2018).

At the same time, since the Basel III accord was promulgated in 2010, the definition of banks' capital has evolved considerably with the purpose of enhancing the stability of the banking system (Bitar et al., 2018). The Basel III agreements notably require the implementation of a regulatory advantage ratio in addition to the weighted capital ratio (Roulette, 2018). Banks have now to strengthen their capitalisation (Churreras et al., 2012). This entails a modification of their balance sheet structure. Indeed, their assets have to be more liquid and their funding more stable. Three capital measures are being considered: capital adequacy ratio, Tier 1 capital ratio and Tier 1 common equity. Holding higher capital ratios can, however, impose constraints on banking activities. In particular it can induce a contraction of credit, which can weaken economic growth, increase risk and reduce the efficiency and profitability of the banking system (Repullo and Suarez, 2012; Olszak et al., 2014). Moreover, capital constraints entail significant contractions of credit (Mésonnier and Monks, 2015; Fraisse et al., 2015; De Jonghe et al., 2016; Mayordomo et al., 2018). Banks are cutting credit to riskier borrowers (Berger and Udell, 1994; Repullo, 2004; Albertazzi and Marchetti, 2010; De Haan and Klomp, 2012). As a result, their non-performing loans are reduced (Barth et al., 2004).

Therefore, liquid and illiquid assets (like loans) are becoming a key issue to discuss profitability and stability of banking institutions (Acharya, Perret and Steffen, 2016). However, there is limited theoretical or empirical research on the effect of minimum liquidity requirements on bank liquidity risk or other risk-taking behaviour (de Young and Jang, 2016). Empirical studies generally use asset and liability ratios rather than liquidity risk ratios (Roulet, 2018). The research has shown that when liquidity variables are significant, their impact on bank lending is positive and significant. This chapter intends to fill this gap by using short and long term debt to evaluate the impact of liquidity on banking market capitalisation.

The question of whether higher capital ratios reduce overall bank risk remains largely unsolved (Fiordelisi et al., 2011). The results are still contradictory (Freixas and Rochet, 2008). In the European context, two studies can be mentioned. Williams (2004) investigated the relationship between non-performing loans, profitability and capital. Poorly managed banks were shown to distribute the worst quality loans. Altunbas et al., (2007), however, were not able to confirm this result. Based on bank loan provisions, profitability and capital, the authors observed that inefficient institutions hold more capital and take on less risk.

These contradictions can be explained partly by the particular nature of the European banking sector. Different ownership structures coexist within the same environment: privately owned stock banks (PO), mutual banks (M) and government-owned (GO) banks (Iannotta et al., 2007).

Mutual banks and public banks are less profitable than private banks, despite their lower operating costs. Public-sector banks provide lower quality loans and have a greater risk of insolvency. Mutual banks offer the soundest loans and present better asset risk ratios than public and private banks. This chapter expands the actual research by constructing a very diversified sample of banking institutions including universal, commercial and cooperative banks to analyse if their business model can influence their credit and liquidity management.

Last but not least, competition and concentration can explain banking fragility. Saif-Alyousfi, A. Y., Saha, A., & Md-Rus, R. (2020) provide evidence in the context of Gulf countries that lower level of competition and lower concentration in the banking market increases the risk-taking behavior of the low capitalized, low liquid and small banks, which add to fragility in the banking system. We could wonder if we could extend this result in the context of European banks.

2.2. Bank Credit Risk Transfer

Asset quality can also be reflected using credit ratings. From the previous literature, a number of authors have identified credit ratings as an important driver of credit risk (Hull et al., 2004, and Karagozoglu and Jacobs, 2010). As such, high credit ratings would be indicative of a better asset quality of the underlying instrument, while a lower credit rating would reflect a riskier asset. Therefore, the growth of credit derivatives and loan sales markets allowed banks to engage more actively in credit risk transfer strategies. The increase in capital and liquidity constraints has further encouraged banking institutions to develop these activities (Beyhaghi et al., 2017). Banks use credit default swaps (CDS) to hedge their exposure to loans and bonds. But they can also trade credit risks (Rodriguèz Gil, 2015).

Basel III regulations allow a bank that uses CDS to reduce its level of regulatory capital. Banks have access to more liquidity and have also easier access to borrowing. The trading of loans helps to increase balance sheet liquidity, and replaces risky assets with cash (Roulet, 2018). However, these practices involve a potential moral hazard. Indeed, lenders may offer loans of poor quality, since they may not need to bear the borrower's credit risk (Martin and Roychowdhury, 2015; Jung and Kim, 2015).

The fact that banks use CDS to transfer risk (Thornton et al., 2018) actually poses three challenges (Cetina et al., 2015). First, transferring risk increases interdependencies between institutions. Systemic risk increases; credit risk turns into counterparty risk, and it becomes difficult to assess the soundness of an institution.

Second, non-banks that are not subject to the same regulations can fully participate in the market. Assessing the ability of these institutions to bear a risk of loss is extremely difficult for a regulator. Finally, Basel III provides an incentive for banks to buy CDS to reduce their regulatory capital, leading to excessive risk taking (Yorulmazer, 2013; Shan et al., 2014; Hasan and Wu, 2016).

For all these reasons, securitisation and trading of credit derivatives have a negative effect on financial stability in Europe (Gonzàlez et al., 2016). Further on, securitisation increases the overall risk of failure of European institutions, as shown by Moody's expected default frequency and z-score measurements (Gonzàlez et al., 2016). One option suggested by some authors is to rely on credit ratings (Hull et al., 2004; Karagozoglu and Jacobs, 2010; Cucinelli et al., 2018) to assess the assets' quality. As asset quality goes up, profitability includes more liquidity, greater risk capacity and a lower cost of funds. This will in turn increase market capitalisation. A summary of the main findings on these issues is provided in the Table below (Table 1).

The aim of our chapter is then to study in depth the capitalisation of European banks by adopting an approach, which distinguishes between short-term challenges and long-term challenges for banks. The ability to refinance short-term debt depends on long-term credit risk profile of banking institutions. Liquidity assessment focuses on the cumulative asset liabilities mismatches and the adequacy of liquid assets to cover maturing liabilities. This justifies our choice to introduce two new variables, which, to the best of our knowledge, have not yet been employed in the literature to date: short-term and long-term debt.

Table 1. Overview of recent results on bank profits, credit practices and risk taking

Authors	Results	Study Period
Profits and Efficiency		
Altunbas et al., 2007	No positive relationship between inefficiency and banks risk-taking in Europe. Inefficient banks hold generally more capital and take less risk.	(1992-2000)
Fiordelisi et al., 2011	Lower bank efficiency with respect to costs and revenues Granger causes higher bank risk. Increases in capital precede cost efficiency improvements in Europe.	(1995-2007)
Chortareas et al., 2012	Strengthening capital restrictions and official supervisory powers can improve the efficient operations of banks in the European Union.	(2000-2008)
Bitar et al., 2018	Risk and non-risk-based capital ratios improve bank efficiency and profitability in 39 OECD countries	(1999-2013)
Credit Risk Transfer and Credit Crunch		
Rodrìguez Gil et al., 2015	European banks that use credit derivatives for hedging experience an improvement in their level of financial stability, while those who opt for a speculative position test negative.	(2006-2010)
Beyhaghi et al., 2017	Banks with capital and liquidity constraints are more likely to use CRT instruments, including CDS.	(2003-2007)
Roulet 2018	The new Basel III capital and liquidity regulations on bank lending have a negative impact on lending growth in Europe.	(2008-2015)
Thornton and di Tommaso 2018	CDS are used for regulatory arbitrage to lower capital requirements and facilitate greater risk taking.	(2001-2016)
Risk		
Iannotta et al., 2007	While ownership concentration does not significantly affect a bank's profitability, a higher ownership concentration is associated with better loan quality, lower asset risk and lower insolvency risk.	(1994-2004)
Gonzalèz et al., 2016	The use of securitization and credit derivatives on the risk profile impacts negatively financial stability.	(2006-2010)
Cucinelli et al., 2018	The introduction of the internal ratings-based approach (IRB) encourages the adoption of stronger risk management practices among banks in Europe.	(2008-2015)

The most recent references are listed in this table, focusing primarily on research related to European banks. A broader review of the literature covering banking regulation and risk in several countries worldwide has been suggested by Bitar et al., 2018.

2.3. Short-Term Debt and Long-Term Debt: A New Perspective

The Basel III liquidity requirements are supposed to increase the amount of liquid assets held by banks and the use of short-term wholesale funding. At the same time, they are intended to limit the extent to which banks can carry out maturity transformation. On the banks' balance sheets, this is reflected in a reorganization of short-term and long-term debt.

On the assets side, if short-term loans increase, the consequences in terms of liquidity will be marked by a reduction in long-term stable financing loans and by an increase in long-term loans, indicating a more stable financing situation. On the liabilities side, a reduction in equity will necessitate an extra source of stable funding to satisfy regulatory requirements. Basel therefore compels banks to shift from liability management to asset management: banks decide to monitor the amount of their assets and search for stable funding to satisfy the capital requirements. This supports the theoretical view of authors such as Motto et al. (2010) and Roger (2011), who advocate for the surplus reserve position required to meet Basel requirements.

Besides stability, there are costs associated with liquidity requirements. Consequently, in a competitive environment, banks tend to finance themselves with less equity and higher debt, largely because more leveraging tends to decrease the cost of capital. In a volatile environment where risk premiums often accompany the quest for funding, a bank is incentivized to issue short-term debt securities, with costs reflective of a strain on liquidity. In periods of liquidity stress, a bank may use its assets to cover cash outflows rather than using the discount slot. As a result, the interest rate on the different sources of funding is a key instrument for ensuring that both Basel III requirements and profitability targets are achieved.

Globally, the contribution of short-term and long-term debt to bank market capitalization reflects a key development in the European banking model. Holding significant levels of short-term debt may be an indicator of the weakness of banking institutions. The banks are compelled to seek out more expensive liquidity, which will influence their risk management. Holding larger volumes of long-term debt is a sign of a more cautious management, which will lower their capitalization level.

3. Data and Research Methodology

We have compiled data for 133 European banks over the period 2000-2017. This information is derived from a Bloomberg terminal. Monthly data have been employed to analyse market indicators, short-term and long-term bank loans, and default probability at 1 and 5 years. Two different panels are investigated. The first one gathers all the financial institutions, while the second one focuses on major banks for comparison purposes. The associated descriptive statistics are included in appendix 3.

3.1. Model

The model retained for our analysis is the following:

$$C_{it} = \alpha_i + \beta(BS)_{it} + \gamma(FM)_{it} + \delta(ECON)_{it} + \varepsilon_{it} \quad (1)$$

where C_{it} is the market capitalization, defined as the total current market value of all of a bank's outstanding shares stated in the pricing currency. $\alpha_i$is a constant, BS gathers balance sheets elements, FM represents financial markets information, ECON retrieves the economic situation and ε is the disturbance term.

Two distinct approaches have been used. The first aims to investigate the role of short-term debt on European bank market capitalisation (C_{it}), while the second focuses on the influence of long-term debt. The explanative variables used are listed in the next table. We used Panel OLS (fixed and random effects) to produce our estimations. The relevance of fixed effects compared to random effects is addressed with Hausman (1978) specification tests.

The most applicable results are then presented.

Table 2. List of Variables

Research Design	**Model 1. Short- term debts impact on Capitalization**	**Model 2. Long-term debts impact on Capitalization**
Balance Sheets (BS)	Return on Assets (ROA) Non-Performing Assets (NPA) Provisions for loans and losses (PLL) Short-term Debt (STD) Tier One Capital Ratio (T1)	Return on Equity (ROE) Non-Performing Loans (NPL) Provisions for loans and losses (PLL) Long-term Debt (LTD) Tier One Capital Ratio (T1)
Financial Markets (FM)	Default Probability 5y. Forward (DP5)[1] Credit Default Swaps spread (CDS)	
Macroeconomic indicators (ECON)	Real GDP (RGDP) Herfindahl Index (HERF)	

As mentioned in this Table, we relate the impact of short-term debt to NPA, and long-term debt to NPL. The rationale for this is the following: NPL reflect a more structural dysfunction and require a long-term oriented operating focus. Non-performing assets, for their part, may significantly affect the banks' published financial statements used by market participants to gauge an institution's return on earnings performance.

Our research hypotheses are consequently as follows:

H1. Capital buffer and CDS spread strongly influence credit risk.

H2. The sector's concentration level has a strong impact on bank market capitalization;

H3. The new regulatory rules reduces the correlation of non-performing loans and the level of market capitalization;

H4. Short-term debts and long-term debts constitute relevant factors that influence market capitalization.

---

[1] In order to prevent co-linearity issues while estimating the models, we have separately considered default probabilities and CDS spreads. Since both variables were highly significant, we only presented the outcomes that were obtained using the CDS spreads.

3.2. A Focus on a Reduced and Representative Panel of Banks

In order to better specify the extent to which regulatory developments influence European banks in the conduct of their activities, we focused our attention on a reduced number of banks (Table 3) and indicators (Appendix A1.). The principal component analysis proposed in this chapter allows doing a comparison between the main European institutions.

Table 3. List of Banks and Average Statistics (%) during the (2003-2016) Period

	ROA	ROE	NPA	PLL	STD	LTD	DP1	DP5
BNP	4,85	8,16	2,99	4,27	4,27	0,00	3,50	4,46
GLE	2,28	3,28	2,40	4,84	4,84	4,25	3,79	3,97
ACA	0,62	0,99	1,41	4,93	4,93	5,98	6,20	5,04
DBK	1,59	4,11	0,78	2,78	2,78	1,93	2,61	0,09
CBK	0,81	0,40	3,64	1,50	1,50	1,85	8,58	6,77
SAN	10,56	10,00	3,79	7,77	7,77	6,10	1,31	3,34
BBVA	**12,36**	**12,97**	4,52	**8,86**	8,86	3,04	1,39	3,39
SAB	10,61	9,38	10,30	8,47	8,47	0,89	2,00	3,92
POP	7,55	6,80	11,20	9,72	**9,72**	5,52	3,64	4,74
BKIA	1,89	-8,07	3,87	1,40	1,40	3,30	3,47	4,63
UCG	2,91	3,67	13,11	7,46	7,46	4,25	7,80	6,29
BP	-3,58	-3,04	**15,55**	7,24	7,24	0,37	**31,25**	**16,59**
MB	5,30	2,90	2,63	5,82	5,82	2,32	1,49	3,20
ISP	5,54	4,31	11,01	6,13	6,13	**21,97**	1,74	3,55
HSBA	4,76	3,96	1,35	2,97	2,97	9,24	1,01	3,09
BARC	1,21	2,31	1,29	3,84	3,84	0,83	3,39	4,43
LLOY	-0,30	-0,48	3,67	3,01	3,01	0,36	2,54	4,35
RBS	-3,81	-6,19	3,03	4,65	4,65	1,54	7,60	5,93
SHBA	9,15	12,58	0,49	0,49	0,49	5,54	1,54	3,44
NDA	10,22	13,46	1,46	1,23	1,23	0,77	1,39	3,32
SWEDA	11,20	12,91	1,12	1,80	1,80	15,74	1,64	3,42
UBSN	4,26	5,58	0,40	0,81	0,81	4,22	2,16	2,01

Source: Bloomberg, Monthly Frequencies (01/01/2003-04/06/2016). Example [12.36]: BBVA is the bank with the highest observed ROA, in average and over the period, in this panel. DP1 stands for 1 year forward default probability.

A small number of the banks investigated – HSBC (United Kingdom), Barclays (United Kingdom), Deutsche Bank (Germany) and UBS

(Switzerland) – are primarily international, as their domestic activities make up less than 50% of their total business. Since most of their business model is internally managed, BNP Paribas (France), Banco Santander (Spain), Unicredit (Italy), Nordea Group (Sweden) and Intesa San Paolo (Italy) are not as widespread as previous institutions. Semi-international banks, such as Royal Bank of Scotland (United Kingdom), BBVA (Spain), Commerzbank (Germany), Svenska and Handelbanken (SHBA) (Sweden), have substantial international operations accounting for 25% to 50% of all their activities.

The last group includes national banks such as Crédit Agricole (France), Lloyds Banking Group (United Kingdom), Société Générale (France), CIC (France), Banco Popolare (Italy), Banco Popular Español (Spain), Commerzbank (Germany), Skandinaviska Enskilda Banken (SEBA) (Sweden) and Swedbank AB (Sweden). Seventy-five percent of their business is domestic. Their business models may influence their resilience to shocks and their vulnerability to systemic risk. The bank with the highest default probability is Banco Popolare, which is consistent with Moody's ratings over this period. This bank reports very small loan loss reserves, and approximately 40% of problem loans. In addition, its position is further weakened by a high level of non-performing assets. BBVA has the highest ROA, which is the result of higher activity in emerging countries and the United States, and lower deposit costs in Spain. Over the same period, the net income of some institutions turned negative because of the crisis period (RBS, Deutsche Bank, and UBS) or the ongoing merger and acquisition operations (Banco Popolare 2011, Intesa San Paolo 2012, Unicredit 2011, Lloyds 2010). Lastly, the absence of long-term debt at BNP Paribas is attributable in part to the fact that the bank uses more fixed-term bonds than long-term loans to refinance its operations.

The average market capitalisation of the banks included in our sample over the period 2003-2016 is 584 billion EUR. The launch of the European banking integration in 2014 has had a considerable impact, costing European banks almost half of their market capitalization (Acharya et al., 2016). As of April 2016, two banks constituted a notable exception: Nordea and Swedbank AB posted very strong market capitalizations. During the second half of 2015, Nordea streamlined its corporate structure by converting its banking affiliates Nordea Bank

Denmark A/S, Nordea Bank Finland Abp and Nordea Bank Norge ASA into Nordea branches. This enabled the company to strengthen its business model and reach a strong market capitalization.

Similarly, the high quality of Swedbank AB's profits ensures an efficient business model and a greater capitalization. The average 5-year CDS spread over the period is 117 bps. Not surprisingly, in the subprime crisis, bank spreads increased sharply. In 2011, BP's five-year CDS spread surpassed 800 bps, while UCG's exceeded 600 bps. Following the crisis, a climate of mistrust towards financial institutions prevailed. Banks, which have assumed a high level of risk, have witnessed a dramatic increase in their CDS spreads, which reflects inefficient risk management.

4. RESULTS

4.1. Panel Analysis

Our results are presented in Tables 4 and 5. We have opted to carry out stepwise panel estimations in order to further investigate the relevance of determining factors of European bank capitalization. The five hypotheses set out in section 3.1 are validated. The most significant outcome, regardless of the model selected, is the relevance of 5 year CDS spreads. This market variable reflects the confidence placed in banking institutions by investors. CDS spreads exhibit a strong negative impact on banks' capitalization over the period under consideration (Hypothesis H1).

The degree of concentration (HERF) in the banking sector also plays an important role in the bank's capitalization process (Hypothesis H2). In particular, a highly-concentrated sector fosters capitalization. It is also worth noting that while the possession of non-performing assets (NPA) triggers an upward capitalization trend; this is not always the case with non-performing loans (NPL). Therefore, the significance of the PLL ratio is lower in the short term than in the long term, as emphasized by Leo de Haan et al., (2016). Banks postpone their provisions for non-performing loans over time, which explains their significance over the long term. Long-term debt corresponds to insured debt. Current regulations have focused on the risks associated to this debt in order to limit its impact on the economy. For its part, short-term debt represents a liquidity risk for the bank. For this reason, regulators have used capital ratios to assess the degree of risk associated with this type of debt.

Table 4. Short-term Debt and European Market Capitalisation: a Stepped-Panel approach

	(1)	(2)	(3)	(4)	(5)	(6)	(7)	(8)	(9)
ROA	1.44***	2.10***	1.93***	1.42***	1.30***	7.57***	6.06***	4.15*	5.73***
	(7.08)	(7.84)	(7.18)	(3.77)	(3.68)	(2.92)	(3.24)	(1.29)	(1.90)
NPA		1.46***	1.75***	1.43**	-3.49	8.48*	1.22***	-2.83	0.06**
		(6.58)	(6.02)	(1.97)	(-0.50)	(1.63)	(2.99)	(-0.5)	(0.31)
PLL			-5.64*	-1.8	2.9	3.19	-2.50	0.27	-0.02
			(-1.59)	(-0.28)	(0.45)	(0.67)	(0.49)	(0.04)	(-0.04)
STD				1.87	-2.42	1.21**	2.86***	1.66***	1.42***
				(0.18)	(-0.28)	(1.77)	(0.52)	(2.43)	(1.93)
T1					1.07***	8.62***	5.03***	7.99***	10.55
					(10.29)	(9.75)	(4.32)	(8.42)	(0.49)
CDS							-1.91***	- 2.24***	-2.51***
							(-3.97)	(-2.39)	(-1.90)
RGDP								-6.8	1.91*
								(-0.76)	(1.69)
HERF									3.59***
									(3.24)
Cst.	8.19***	7.99***	8.09***	8.44***	-2.43	7.34	5.36***	2.90***	2.12***
	(51.61)	(48.72)	(45.52)	(9.38)	(-0.33)	(1.12)	(4.79)	(3.05)	(4.43)
R. Sq.	0.9272	0.9586	0.9583	0.9608	0.5681	0.7350	0.9902	0.8025	0.9956
Hausman	24.87***	59.74***	75.46***	32.22***	6.70	3.81	13.62**	5.84	13.77**
Reg. under	FE	FE	FE	FE	RE	RE	FE	RE	FE

Fixed effects (FE) or Random effects (RE) Panel OLS. Values of t-test in brackets, ***$p < 0.01$; **$p < 0.05$; *$p < 0.1$. The short-term debt variable is made up of bonds or other debt instruments that mature within the next five years. Also included are balance sheet liabilities with maturities of less than one year. The item includes demand deposits, discounted bills, and amounts due to other banks or financial institutions. We report the results using ROA and non-performing assets in these models since ROE and non-performing loans did not return any significance when tested. In cases where the Hausman test failed to validate the relevance of a fixed-effects approach (Models 1, 5, 6, and 8), the results using random effects are reported in the table for comparison purposes.

Table 5. Long-term Debt and European Market Capitalisation: a Stepped-Panel approach

	(1)	(2)	(3)	(4)	(5)	(6)	(7)	(8)	(9)
ROE	1.58***	1.71***	1.46***	1.35***	1.11***	0.75***	0.61***	0.80***	0.92***
	(7.36)	(5.77)	(4.85)	(4.62)	(3.80)	(3.66)	(3.22)	(2.71)	(3.23)
NPL		1.02*	1.78**	1.28*	-4.35	-1.57	1.74	1.39	0.56
		(3.40)	(4.89)	(3.49)	(-0.80)	(-0.41)	(0.47)	(0.29)	(1.25)
PLL			-1.40***	-1.65***	-2.02***	-0.81***	-0.58***	-1.01***	-0.79***
			(-3.74)	(-4.45)	(-4.94)	(-2.78)	(-2.07)	(-2.19)	(-1.94)
LTD				1.72***	1.06	-0.07	0.05	0.30***	0.56***
				(5.58)	(0.19)	(-0.19)	(0.15)	(0.59)	(1.24)
T1					5.40***	5.81***	7.61***	8.00***	9.66***
					(5.42)	(8.34)	(9.27)	(7.49)	(13.18)
CDS							-2.15***	-2.11***	-1.58***
							(-5.83)	(-4.32)	(-2.91)
RGDP								2.27	1.21
								(0.64)	(0.35)
HERF									8.87***
									(2.95)
Cst.	7.79***	8.11***	8.39***	7.22***	5.78***	5.92***	4.26***	3.97***	4.18***
	(47.40)	(29.55)	(29.24)	(20.47)	(7.55)	(11.12)	(6.13)	(4.41)	(5.03)
R. Sq.	0.4679	0.9605	0.9615	0.9646	0.9668	0.9846	0.9873	0.9843	0.8537
Hausman	0.70	73.06***	89.02***	128.53***	84.52***	70.88***	22.83***	17.08***	11.70
Reg. under	RE	FE	FE	FE	FE	FE	FE	FE	RE

Fixed effects (FE) or Random effects (RE) Panel OLS. Values of t-test in brackets, ***$p < 0.01$; **$p < 0.05$; *$p < 0.1$. The long-term debt variable covers debt securities with a term of more than 5 years generally accompanied by interest payments. We report the results using ROE and non-performing loans in these models since ROA and non-performing assets did not return any significance when tested. In cases where the Hausman test failed to validate the relevance of a fixed-effects approach (Models 1 and 9), the results using random effects are reported in the table for comparison purposes.

The difference we achieve in our findings between NPAs and NPLs illustrates the usefulness, at least in part, of the prudential regulations in place. Indeed, Basel III has enabled credit risk to be better managed, thanks to its recent developments. NPLs no longer have a substantial impact on market capitalization. The application of qualitative factors to classify large, wholesale exposures as “nonperforming” in the NPA will influence more strongly capitalization and therefore would allow supervisors to place exposures in the NPA more than in NPL.

Regulatory developments have led banks to raise their provisions to hedge the credit risk associated with the presence of NPL on their balance sheets. But this is also why, as Daru (2016) states, NPAs have a direct impact on the bank's liquidity position and on their market capitalization. This striking outcome is in line with the findings of Bourke (1989). This also justify why regulatory authorities intend to detect prudential provisioning shortfalls, to restore banking stability.

In addition, the finding indicates that despite the importance of T1 and therefore of European prudential regulation; banks remain exposed to defaults on the loans they issue (Hypothesis H3).

Finally, the debt structure of European banking institutions, both short-term (STD) and long-term (LTD), has an impact on the development of market capitalization over time (Hypothesis H4). The two key profitability ratios (ROA and ROE) used in our estimates are highly significant in all the models tested.

4.2. Analysis a Cluster of Representative Banks

As explained in section 3, we complemented our panel analysis with an examination focused on a set of selected representative banks from our initial sample. These banks are significantly involved in the market but do not have identical business models (see section 3.2). The aim is therefore first to study possible similarities in their positioning, and then to establish representative clusters of banks using data analytics.

The purpose of this heatmap, which is derived from the average correlations between the parameters displayed in Table 3, is to visualize the banks with opposing business models. In the red cluster, there is a small group of institutions that are opposed to a large majority of banks (negative correlation thresholds ranging from 60 to 90%). These institutions are Bankia, Royal Bank of Scotland, Banco Popolare (BKIA, RBS, BP), Lloyds and to a lesser extent Crédit Agricole and Commerzbank (ACA and CZB).

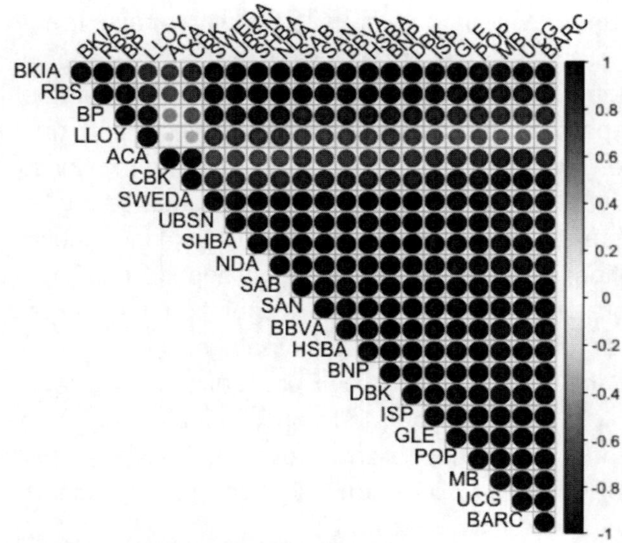

Source: Bloomberg, Monthly frequencies, in average over the (2003-2016) period.

Figure 1. Correlation Heatmap between Banks.

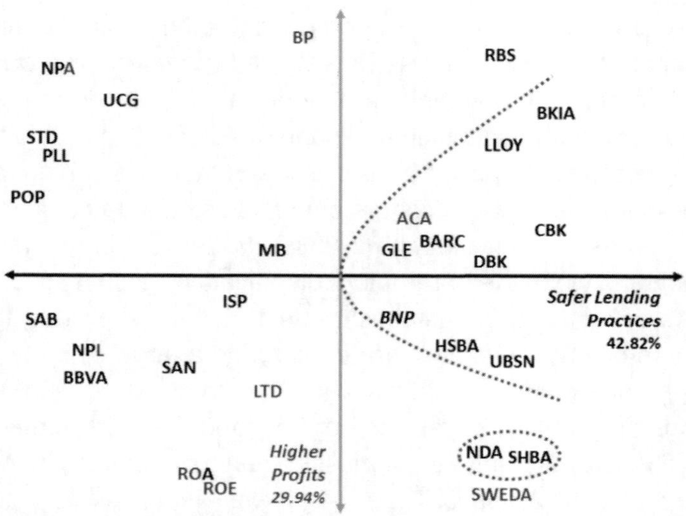

Principal Component Analysis, Cumulative Proportion of Information on Axes: 72.76%.

Figure 2. Average Positioning of European Banks during the (2003-2016) Period.

These institutions are all members of the last group of banks outlined in Section 3.2. The business model of these banks is mainly based on their domestic market. For all the other banks that operate beyond national borders (blue cluster), the correlation ranges from 60 to 87%. Consequently, their business models appear to be quite close. In order to confirm this result, we used a principal component analysis. This enables us to identify clusters with representative practices. The contributions and squared cosines per bank, as well as their correlations with axes, are provided in Appendix 3 and 4. The resulting mapping is displayed in Figure 2.

The set of variables used for this empirical study are relevant for the mapping, with the exception of default probabilities and CDS spreads. All the others exhibit significant correlation with one axis, meaning that while some proximity (relevant in the case of profitability indicators such as ROA and ROE), each one can be used to categorize the practices within each of the bank groups. Two different axes can thus be defined. The first one represents the capacity of institutions to be profitable, whereas the second one illustrates the safest lending practices. As a result, there are clear oppositions: the banks with significant amounts of non-performing assets (NPA) are the ones with the lowest profits.

The banks with the soundest credit practices are distancing themselves from those institutions where profits are in some cases larger, but for which long-term debts (LTD) and non-performing loans (NPL) are the biggest. It is worth noting that it is not a bank's scope of operations (domestic or international) that will affect its location in this mapping. That is, a bank may conduct most of its business domestically and still fall into the group that has, on average, the safest lending practices. Indeed, the group on the right contains both BNP and Lloyds. The business model of banks is thus mainly defined by the way banks handle their assets (NPA) and debts (STD and LTD), which is consistent with our previous comments.

Conclusion

The purpose of this chapter was to identify the drivers of the market capitalization of European banks in a transition context related to the implementation of the European banking integration. A first step consisted in carrying out step-by-step panel estimations to identify the key factors contributing to banking capitalisation. To this end, a distinction has been suggested regarding the nature of the debt carried by banks. Two separate models were thus thoroughly examined. A second step involved focusing on a smaller sample of representative banks. This allowed us to investigate the differences between institutions that were originally assumed to have similar business models.

A first result obtained in this chapter concerns investors' evaluation of the resilience of banking institutions. The ability of banks to fulfil their commitments on the financial market, as well as the confidence that is placed in them through dedicated financing operations constitute key factors that significantly affect capitalisation. In addition to the regulatory rules that restrict banking activities, our results emphasize the importance for banks to enhance their efficiency in terms of both stability and profitability in order to determine the adequate level of capitalization. The alignment between these two factors will reflect their business model, as outlined in our cluster analysis.

A second result achieved in this chapter relates to the structure of the debt owned by European banking institutions. In the short-term and the long-term, these debts significantly influence bank capitalization. In addition, the reduced sample analysis confirmed that the banks with the safest credit practices on average are not the ones with the highest profits and debts. The more profitable institutions hold the highest levels of long-term debt, and the largest share of non-performing loans. The most vulnerable institutions are the ones with significant levels of short-term debt and large volumes of non-performing assets. Regulators require that banks hold higher capital buffers to guarantee the stability of the financial system.

A bank's approach to financing now provides clues to understanding its business model. By focusing on asset management rather than liability management, banks are increasing advantage, which influence the debt cost.

A third result highlights that although the increase in non-performing assets typically involves an extra capitalization effort by banks, this is not the case with non-performing loans. There is thus room for banking prudential regulation to further evolve, beyond the traditional capital requirements.

A fourth result from this work indicates that it is not the activities of a bank abroad that will influence its capitalization capacities or its management practices. It is rather the trade-off between the structure of short-term and long-term debt that provides a clearer picture of the business model of banks.

References

Acharya V. V., D. Perret, and Steffen, S. (2016). Capital shortfalls of European Banks since the Start of the Banking Union, *Working Paper*, NYU, July 27.

Albertazzi, U., & Marchetti, D. J. (2010). Credit supply, flight to quality and evergreening: an analysis of bank-firm relationships after Lehman. *Bank of Italy Temi di Discussione (Working Paper) No*, *756*.

Altunbas, Y., Carbo, S., Gardener, E. P., & Molyneux, P. (2007). Examining the relationships between capital, risk and efficiency in European banking. *European Financial Management*, *13*(1), pp. 49-70.

Barth, J. R., G. Caprio, J R., and R. Levine (2004). Bank regulation and supervision: What works best? *Journal of Financial Intermediation*, 13, 205–248.

Berger, A. N. (1995). The Relationship between Capital and Earnings in Banking. *Journal of Money Credit and Banking* 27, pp. 432-456.

Berger, A. N., & Sedunov, J. (2017). Bank liquidity creation and real economic output. *Journal of Banking & Finance*, *81*, pp. 1-19.

Berger, A. N. and C. H. S. Bouwman (2013). How does capital affect bank performance during financial crises? *Journal of Financial Economics*, 109, pp. 146–176.

Berger, A. N. and G. F. Udell (1994). Did risk-based capital allocate bank credit and cause a “credit crunch” in the United States? *Journal of Money, Credit and Banking*, 26, pp. 585–628.

Beyhaghi M., Massoud N., & Saunders A., (2017). Why and how do banks lay off credit risk? The choice between retention, loan sales and credit default swaps, *Journal of Corporate Finance*, 42, pp. 335-355.

Bharath, S. T., & Shumway, T. (2008). Forecasting default with the Merton distance to default model. *Review of Financial Studies*, *21*(3), pp. 1339-1369.

Bitar, M., Pukthuanthong K., & Walker T., (2018). The effect of capital ratios on the risk, efficiency and profitability of banks: Evidence from OECD countries, *Journal of International Financial Markets, Institutions and Money*, 53, pp. 227-262.

Bourke, P. (1989). Concentration and other determinants of bank profitability in Europe, North America and Australia. *Journal of Banking & Finance*, 13(1), pp. 65-79.

Cai, L., and R. Singenellore, (2015). "Bloomberg Credit Default Risk for private Companies: Framework, Methodology & Usage," *Bloomberg Professional Service*, DRSK, Bloomberg Finance L. P., BFLP.

Cetina, J., & Gleason, K. I. (2015). The difficult business of measuring banks' liquidity: Understanding the liquidity coverage ratio. *Office of Financial Research Working Paper*, (15-20).

Chortareas, G. E., Girardone, C., & Ventouri, A. (2012). Bank supervision, regulation, and efficiency: Evidence from the European Union. *Journal of Financial Stability*, *8*(4), pp. 292-302.

Cucinelli, D., Di Battista M. L., Marchese M. & Nieri L., (2018), Credit risk in European Banks: The bright side of the Internal Ratings based approach, *Journal of Banking & Finance,* in press.

de Haan, L. and M. RC Van Oordt. (2018) "Timing of banks' loan loss provisioning during the crisis." *Journal of Banking & Finance* 87, pp. 293-303.

Daru, M. U. (2016). NPA in Banking Sector: As an Indicator of Financial Inefficiency. *International Journal of Research in Finance and Marketing*, *6*(12), pp. 132-139.

De Jonghe, O., Dewachter, H., & Ongena, S. (2016). *Bank capital (requirements) and credit supply: Evidence from pillar 2 decisions* (No. 303). Working Paper Research.

DeYoung, R., & Jang, K. Y. (2016). Do banks actively manage their liquidity?. *Journal of Banking & Finance*, *66*, pp. 143-161.

Fiordelisi, F., Marques-Ibanez, D., & Molyneux, P. (2011). Efficiency and risk in European banking. *Journal of Banking & Finance*, *35*(5), pp. 1315-1326.

Fraisse, H., M. Le, M. and D. Thesmar (2015). The real effects of bank capital requirements, Unpublished Working Paper.

Freixas, X., & Rochet, J. C. (2008). *Microeconomics of banking*. MIT press.

González, L. O., Gil, L. I. R., Cunill, O. M., & Lindahl, J. M. M. (2016). The effect of financial innovation on European banks' risk. *Journal of Business Research*, *69*(11), pp. 4781-4786.

Hausman, J. A. (1978). Specification tests in econometrics. *Econometrica: Journal of the econometric society*, pp. 1251-1271.

Hull, J., C., Predescu, M., and White, A., (2004). The Relationship between credit default swap spread spreads, bond yields, and credit rating announcements. *Journal of Banking and Finance*, 28, pp. 2789-2811.

Iannotta, G., Nocera, G., & Sironi, A. (2007). Ownership structure, risk and performance in the European banking industry. *Journal of Banking & Finance*, *31*(7), pp. 2127-2149.

Karagozoglu, A., and Jacobs, M., (2010), Measuring Credit Risk: CDS Spreads vs. Credit Ratings. *Working Paper, Office of the Comptroller of the Currency and the U.S. Department of Treasury.*

Kim, D., & Santomero, A. M. (1988). Risk in banking and capital regulation. *The Journal of Finance*, *43*(5), pp. 1219-1233.

Klomp, J., & De Haan, J. (2012). Banking risk and regulation: Does one size fit all? *Journal of Banking & Finance*, *36*(12), pp. 3197-3212.

Martin, X., & Roychowdhury, S. (2015). Do financial market developments influence accounting practices? Credit default swaps and borrowers' reporting conservatism. *Journal of Accounting and Economics*, *59*(1), pp. 80-104.

Mayordomo, S., & Rodriguez-Moreno, M. (2018). *How Do European Banks Cope with Macroprudential Capital Requirements?*

Merton, Robert C. (1974). On the pricing of corporate debt: The risk structure of interest rates. *The Journal of finance* 29.2, pp. 449-470.

Mésonnier, J. S., & Monks, A. (2014). *Did the EBA capital exercise cause a credit crunch in the euro area?*

Motto, R., Rostagno, M., & Christiano, L. J. (2010). Financial factors in economic fluctuations. In *2010 Meeting Papers* (No. 141). Society for Economic Dynamics.

Olszak, M., Pipien, M., Roszkowska, S., & Kowalska, I. (2014). The effects of capital on bank lending in large EU banks–the role of procyclicality, income smoothing, regulations and supervision. *University of Warsaw Faculty of Management Working Paper*, (5).

Paulet, E. M. Parnaudeau and T. Abdessemed, (2014). "The SME Struggle for Financing: A Clampdown in European Banks Post-Crisis," *Journal of Business Strategy*, 35(2), pp. 36-45.

Paulet, E. M. Parnaudeau and T. Abdessemed, (2015) Cooperative versus commercial banking strategies in Europe after the subprime crisis: the alternative choice between profitability and stability, ***5th*** In *Banking: Services, Opportunities and Risks* Kazik Jerzy Editor Nova pp. 157-184.

Repullo, R. (2004). Capital requirements, market power, and risk-taking in banking. *Journal of financial Intermediation*, *13*(2), pp. 156-182.

Repullo, R., & Suarez, J. (2012). The procyclical effects of bank capital regulation. *The Review of financial studies*, *26*(2), pp. 452-490.

Roger, S. and J. Vlček, (2011), Macroeconomic Costs of Higher Bank Capital and Liquidity Requirements (May 2011). *IMF Working Papers*, Vol., pp. 1-51, 2011. Available at SSRN: https://ssrn.com/abstract=1847336.

Roulet, C., (2018). Basel III: Effects of capital and liquidity regulations on European bank lending, *Journal of Economics and Business*, 95, pp. 26-46.

Saif-Alyousfi, A. Y., Saha, A., & Md-Rus, R. (2020). The impact of bank competition and concentration on bank risk-taking behavior and stability: Evidence from GCC countries. *The North American Journal of Economics and Finance*, *51*, 100867.

Staikouras, C., Mamatzakis, E., Koutsomanoli-Filippaki. A. (2008). An empirical investigation of operating performance in the new European banking landscape. *Global Finance Journal,* 19, 32-45.

Uhde, A., Heimeshoff, U. (2009). Consolidation in banking and financial stability in Europe: Empirical evidence. *Journal of Banking & Finance,* 33, 1299-1311.

Thornton, J. and di Tommaso, C., (2018). *Credit Default Swaps and Regulatory Capital relief: Evidence from European Banks*, Finance Research Letters, in Press.

Yorulmazer, T. (2013). Has financial innovation made the world riskier? CDS, regulatory arbitrage and systemic risk. *CDS, Regulatory Arbitrage and Systemic Risk (April 23, 2013)*.

APPENDIX A1. LIST OF RATIOS

Ratio	Measure	Signification	Definition
Capital requirement (also known as regulatory capital or capital adequacy) is the amount of capital a bank has to hold as required by the regulator.	Tier1 Risk based capital ratio	Stability of the banking system	This is usually expressed as a capital adequacy ratio of equity that must be held as a percentage of risk-weighted assets.
Asset quality	Non-performing loans/ total loans and non-performing assets/total assets	Risk management	Non-performing assets are stressed assets, advances, where interest and/or instalment of principal remain overdue for a period of more than 90 days in respect to the term.
Profitability	ROA	Profitability	ROA tends to tell us how effectively an organization is taking earnings advantage of its base of assets.
Default probability 5 year	Combines information on capital structure (Total assets to total liabilities and Book equity to current liabilities), on liquidity (cash/current liabilities), on profitability (ROA et ROE), on market fluctuations, and on solvency probability to obtain the year default probability	Market Risk	These indexes indicate the probability of default 5 years forward and 1 year forward. These measures are based on the propositions of of Merton (1974), Bharath and Shumway (2008), and lastly Altman and Sabato (2005). See also Cai and Singenellore (2015) for the complete methodology.
Default probability 1 year			

Appendix A1. (Continued)

Ratio	Measure	Signification	Definition
Short term debt	Includes bank overdrafts, short-term debts and borrowings, repurchase agreements (repos) and reverse repos, short-term portion of long-term borrowings.	Potential fragility of banking institution	The lower the short-term debt, the higher the stability for banks
Long-term debt	All interest-bearing financial obligations that are not due within a year. Includes convertible, redeemable, retractable debentures, bonds, loans, mortgage debts, sinking funds, and long-term bank overdrafts. Excludes short-term portion of long-term debt, pension obligations, deferred tax liabilities and preferred equity.	Systemic banking risk	The long-term debt ratio evaluates the resolvability of systemic banking firms, reduces the threat to financial stability.
Loan Loss Provisions	This provision is used to cover potential loan losses like bad loans, customer defaults and renegotiated terms of a loan. An adjustment to loan loss reserves, they are also known as valuation allowances.	Systemic banking risk	It measures the costs the bank has set aside for future losses on loans

Appendix A2. Descriptive Statistics

	CMC	ROA	ROE	NPA	NPL	PLL
Mean	14625.73	1.41	7.10	9123.794	10773.16	1044.526
Median	2381.507	0.58	8.26	4169.000	5776.000	150.500
Std. Dev.	34128.60	7.42	19.93	13077.34	13694.94	2437.987
	STD	**LTD**	**DP5**	**CDS**	**RGDP**	**HERF**
Mean	29758.78	36410.16	0.023	588.91	1.166	0.0481
Median	10274.33	2708.548	0.018	80.00	1.500	0.045
Std. Dev.	45745.40	97941.35	0.022	17238.62	1.909	0.0076

Appendix A3. Contributions and Squared Cosines

		Axis 1		Axis 2	
		Ctr	*Cos2*	*Ctr*	*Cos2*
1	BNP	*0.1606004*	*0.07224297*	*1.845527e-01*	*5.806218e-02*
2	GLE	**0.2829572**	**0.25447505**	3.117921e-01	1.961162e-01
3	ACA	0.6459968	0.22077052	**1.027088e+00**	**2.454948e-01**
4	DBK	**3.0302152**	**0.82879114**	9.290703e-03	1.777232e-03
5	CBK	**5.0050975**	**0.80621125**	7.318460e-01	8.244796e-02
6	SAN	**4.0666936**	**0.49103590**	2.002211e+00	1.690852e-01
7	BBVA	**9.1636859**	**0.60626332**	3.110911e+00	1.439470e-01
8	SAB	**23.7159574**	**0.71903862**	8.908927e-01	1.889126e-02
9	POP	**19.2502569**	**0.97679403**	2.572961e-01	9.131109e-03
10	BKIA	**5.8894426**	**0.50336655**	3.188130e+00	1.905768e-01
11	UCG	**4.2517630**	**0.45182859**	4.577917e+00	3.402487e-01
12	BP	0.9393834	0.04151150	**2.601601e+01**	**8.040633e-01**
13	MB	**1.0752873**	**0.24696724**	2.227864e-05	3.578718e-06
14	ISP	**2.9876766**	**0.13823704**	6.362712e-02	2.059003e-03
15	HSBA	**1.5713270**	**0.47167223**	7.989412e-01	1.677307e-01
16	BARC	**1.7092018**	**0.54479595**	6.547325e-01	1.459581e-01
17	LLOY	**2.8154758**	**0.54867918**	2.713078e+00	3.697881e-01
18	RBS	**2.1795338**	*0.19386238*	1.151012e+01	**7.160340e-01**
19	SHBA	**3.5211708**	*0.28316293*	1.170421e+01	**6.582870e-01**
20	NDA	**1.2775298**	*0.10858027*	1.068530e+01	**6.351708e-01**
21	SWEDA	0.6946170	0.03987687	**1.792736e+01**	**7.198067e-01**
22	UBSN	**5.7661302**	**0.80663555**	1.634675e+00	1.599367e-01

Italics: not properly represented on axes; Bold: Significantly repr. on this axis.

Appendix A4. Correlation to Axis

	Corr to Axis 1	p.value
STD	0.9194895	1.476693e-09
PLL	0.9194895	1.476693e-09
NPL	0.6973204	3.097986e-04
NPA	0.6930267	3.495569e-04
ROA	0.4569448	3.252266e-02
	Corr to Axis 2	**p.value**
ROE	0.8655262	1.980217e-07
ROA	0.8645095	2.125725e-07
NPA	-0.4984498	1.822056e-02

INDEX

G

H

I

L

M

N

O

P

R

S

T

U

V

W